**Learn HOW to worship Him.**

The "songs heard around the throne" in the Book of Revelation provide a foretaste of the glorious praise you will give to the King of Kings in the hereafter. In this book, Robert E. Coleman shows you how to enter that same dimension of worship, *here and now*. *Songs of Heaven* offers you insight into the cryptic symbolism of Revelation, as well as practical experience in learning new ways to praise and adore your King.

*"To get the most from the book, let me suggest that you try to bring the songs into your own quiet moments of prayer.... I know of no more uplifting exercise to the soul. After all, these hymns are sung in the Presence of the King, and we have every right to join the celebration."*

—The author

BY Robert E. Coleman

*Established by the Word of God*
*Introducing the Prayer Cell*
*Life in the Living Word*
*The Master Plan of Evangelism*
*The Spirit and the Word*
*Dry Bones Can Live Again*
*One Divine Moment,* Editor
*Written in Blood*
*Evangelism in Perspective*
*The Mind of the Master*
*They Meet the Master*
*Songs of Heaven*

# Songs of Heaven

## Robert E. Coleman

Fleming H. Revell Company
Old Tappan, New Jersey

Unless otherwise identified, Scripture quotations in this volume are from the New American Standard Bible, Copyright © THE LOCKMAN FOUNDATION 1960, 1962, 1963, 1968, 1971, 1972, 1973, 1975 and are used by permission.

Scripture quotations identified PHILLIPS are from THE NEW TESTAMENT IN MODERN ENGLISH (Revised Edition), translated by J. B. Phillips. © J. B. Phillips 1958, 1960, 1972. Used by permission of Macmillan Publishing Co., Inc.

Scripture quotations identified NIV are from HOLY BIBLE New International Version, copyright ©, New York International Bible Society, 1978. Used by permission.

**Library of Congress Cataloging in Publication Data**
Coleman, Robert Emerson, date
  Songs of heaven.
  Includes bibliographical references.
  1. Bible. N. T. Revelation—Criticism,
interpretation, etc. I. Title.
BS2825.2.C57    228'.06    80-450
ISBN-0-8007-1107-6  Hardback
ISBN 0-8007-5097-7    Power Book

TO Mom and Dad,
who heightened in me a desire
to sing with the angels

Come, ye that love the Saviour's name,
  And joy to make it known,
The Sov'reign of your hearts proclaim,
  And bow before his throne.

Behold your Lord, your Master, crown'd
  With glories all divine:
And tell the wond'ring nations round,
  How bright those glories shine.

When, in his earthly courts, we view
  The glories of our King,
We long to love as angels do,
  And wish, like them, to sing.

And shall we long and wish in vain?
  Lord, teach our songs to rise:
Thy love can animate the strain,
  And bid it reach the skies.

                              ANNE STEELE

# Contents

Crown Him with many crowns,
    The Lamb upon His throne:
Hark! how the heavenly anthem drowns
    All music but its own!
Awake, my soul, and sing
    Of Him who died for thee,
And hail Him as thy matchless King
    Through all eternity.

Crown Him the Lord of life:
    Who triumphed o'er the grave,
And rose victorious to the strife
    For those He came to save;
His glories now we sing,
    Who died and rose on high,
Who died eternal life to bring
    And lives that death may die.

Crown Him of lords the Lord,
    Who over all doth reign,
Who once on earth, the Incarnate Word,
    For ransomed sinners slain,
Now lives in realms of light,
    Where saints with angels sing
Their songs before Him day and night,
    Their God, Redeemer, King.

Crown Him the Lord of heaven:
    Enthroned in worlds above;
Crown Him the King, to whom is given
    The wondrous name of Love.
Crown Him with many crowns,
    As thrones before Him fall,
Crown Him, ye kings, with many crowns,
    For He is King of all.

MATTHEW BRIDGES

*11*

# Introduction: Learning the Language of Heaven

Come, Thou Fount of every blessing,
   Tune my heart to sing Thy grace;
Streams of mercy, never ceasing,
   Call for songs of loudest praise.
Teach me some melodious sonnet,
Sung by flaming tongues above. . . .

ROBERT ROBINSON

## The Gladsome Sound

On Easter morning, 1799, the Austrian citizens of Feldkirch awoke to find their peaceful village besieged by the army of Napoleon. Knowing that the town's defenses could not withstand an attack, those in authority hastily called a meeting, to decide if they should hoist the white flag in surrender to the enemy.

The dean of the church rose first and addressed the somber assembly. "This is Easter Day," he said in a trembling voice. "This is the day of our King's Resurrection. We must have one moment of triumph. Let us at least ring the bells. If the town falls, it falls; but we must ring all the bells of Easter."

His counsel prevailed, and soon, from the church towers, the bells rang out their joyous sound; the vibrant music reverberated through the valleys and hills of Feldkirch, filling the frosty air with gladness.

The invaders, massed outside the gate, were confounded. Why should there be such celebration? Concluding that the

Austrian army had arrived during the night to relieve the town, the French broke camp and were in full retreat before the bells stopped ringing.[1]

In a more profound way, the church today, like that mountain hamlet, is under siege by a mighty adversary. Powers and principalities of far-reaching influence seek to destroy the city of God by every devious means; as the end of the age approaches, these forces of evil can be expected to become more brazen and defiant in their deadly assault. Viewed from a purely human perspective, the cause of righteousness would seem doomed and the disciples of Christ defeated.

But God's people do not see the conflict from the vantage point of the world, or measure resources by the wisdom and strength of man. We belong to another country—a city not made with hands. When we perceive our present struggles in the light of this higher reality, it is not strange that sounds of victory should rise above the strife. Whatever may be our experience in this present age, we know that the kingdom of Christ shall never perish.

A man was asked if he expected to go to heaven when he died. "Why," he replied, "I *live* there." Indeed, for the Christian, this is true. In the deepest sense of our spiritual beings, since we are in Christ Jesus, we sit with Him in heaven (Eph. 2:6; cf. Eph. 1:3; Eph. 3:10; Col. 3:1,2). There we already have "our citizenship" (Phil. 3:20). His inheritance is our possession now, by faith (Eph. 1:11,14,18; Titus 2:14; Col. 1:12), for the future is present in Him who is ever the same, "yesterday and today, yes and forever" (Heb. 13:8).

---

[1] Adapted from "The Triumph of the Bells," a gem from the Coronet Story Teller by Rev. Philip Cleveland, *Coronet*, November 1948, p. 154. Though this account is only legendary, one may find mention of the repulse of the French attack in historical records.

## The Revelation of the Victor

One of the most beautiful ways to contemplate what life in Him means is to read the Book of Revelation. Given by God to show His servants what will take place (1:1),[2] the account is an unveiling of the reigning Christ,[3] as He lives in His church; it depicts His conquest over every kind of opposition and the establishment of His eternal kingdom. While much of the narrative concerns the destructive work of evil on the earth and the consequent judgments that fall upon the wicked, attention centers upon Him who sits upon the throne of heaven,[4] the Lord, high and lifted up, directing the unfolding destiny of man according to His own purpose.

In His throne form, God reigns in unapproachable splendor and power. He is always represented as being seated (a mode of expressing His authority and dominion), undisturbed by the conflict raging beneath Him. When the angels step forth, as His messengers, to proclaim some new chapter in His cosmic plan, "We do not even see a movement of His hand, giving them the word of command; the command comes by voice alone—God Himself remains hidden, in untouched holy majesty."[5]

---

[2] All Scripture references in which a book is not indicated are from the Book of Revelation.

[3] The word *revelation* or *Apocalypse* means disclosure of something previously hidden. In the New Testament, it usually describes God's self-disclosure of truth to man, implying divine initiative. As the term is used in this introductory verse, it is "The Revelation of Jesus Christ," which could mean that it was made by Him, or about Him, or that it is His possession. Perhaps all three aspects pertain. In any case, the book cannot be separated from the Person of Christ.

[4] As an indication of the centrality of this theme, the word for *throne* occurs forty-six times in the book, while related words, which emphasize the same sovereign reign of God—such as authority, power, rule, kingdom, and king—occur seventy-seven times.

[5] Hanns Lilje, *The Last Book of the Bible*, trans. Olive Wyon (Philadelphia: Muhlenberg Press, 1957), p. 14.

He is introduced as the eternal One, "who is and who was and who is to come"; the Spirit, in His infinite perfection; "and . . . Jesus Christ, the faithful witness, the firstborn of the dead, and the ruler of the kings of the earth" (1:4,5).[6] Only in His incarnate form, as "one like a son of man," is His accessibility to us recognized. Even in this manifestation, the sight is so awesome that the writer, typifying the attitude of the reverent reader, falls at His feet as a dead man, and not until approached by the Lord is he able to continue (1:13–16; cf. 19:10–16). "Do not be afraid," Jesus says, "I am the first and the last, and the living One; and I was dead, and behold, I am alive forevermore, and I have the keys of death and of Hades" (1:17,18). This is He who "is coming with the clouds, and every eye will see Him, even those who pierced Him; and all the tribes of the earth will mourn over Him. . . . the Lord God . . . Almighty" (1:7,8).

In the revelation of His majesty there is also the unveiling of His redemption. For this mighty God, who created the worlds by His word, the Sovereign of the universe, before whom empires tremble and nations fall, the Potentate of glory, "loves us, and released us from our sins by His blood, and He has made us to be a kingdom, priests to His God and Father." The realization is too wonderful to express. Before such grace, one can only fall down and say, "to Him be the glory and the dominion forever and ever. Amen" (1:5,6).

## Worship in Song

What is seen in this early doxology reflects the spirit of adoration resounding through the whole Revelation, particu-

---

[6] The nature of the Trinity, as noted here, is not explained throughout the Revelation, though the Persons of the Godhead can be recognized. This follows the pattern of Scripture, which enhances the mystery of the divine Being, while stressing the reality.

larly in the songs heard around the throne.[7] Beginning in chapter 4 and continuing intermittently through chapter 19, these paeans of praise provide a celestial background to history that, amid the dissolution of human institutions, "abides the unchanging reality of an eternal world in which God's purpose is unfailing and in which His Christ is victorious."[8]

More personally, they disclose the proper response of created beings to the glory of God. Worship is the essence: not the giddy, sentimental feelings of nostalgia seen in much modern expression, but the real stuff of devotion—the kind of intelligent love that offers itself to God as a sacrifice of thanksgiving. The joy of martyrdom is in it—the pouring out of life to Him who alone is worthy. While not depreciating human experience, the songs about the throne are occupied with a greater theme: God is their object—His character, His attributes, His acts, His benefits, His pleasure—and it is in beholding His glory that the creature has its highest joy. These songs, then, can be said to represent the language of heaven. Indeed, in the presence of the throne, nothing else seems appropriate.

Some historians believe that these hymns, or portions of them, were actually sung by the early Christians and thereby became a part of their service of worship.[9] There is no doubt

---

[7] They are called songs because of the nature of the address to God. Actually, most of the passages refer to speaking, rather than singing, especially when alluding to angelic beings. However, the word for speaking is consistent with singing, so that all can be so regarded. Leon Morris, *The Revelation of St. John* (Grand Rapids: Wm. B. Eerdmans, 1969), p. 100.

[8] Merrill C. Tenney, *Interpreting Revelation* (Grand Rapids: Wm. B. Eerdmans, 1957), p. 37.

[9] *See* Ralph P. Martin, *Worship in the Early Church* (Grand Rapids: Wm. B. Eerdmans, 1974), pp. 42–46; Lucetta Moury, "Revelation 4–5 and Early Christian Liturgical Usage," *Journal of Biblical Literature*

that they have characteristics of the earliest liturgical hymns, particularly those found in the Psalms, which may have influenced their composition. Although John wrote what he saw, this fact does not preclude the possibility of his visions incorporating established patterns of worship in the church, just as he freely used the old norms of Scripture.

The poet Carlyle wrote: "Let me make a nation's songs, and I care not who makes their laws."[10] His point is well-taken, for those things we spontaneously sing about, more than anything else, have a way of shaping our minds, just as, in time, they reveal what is uppermost in our thoughts. So it is with the songs about the throne. They express the deepest desires of those who, with unveiled face, have seen the Lord in His glory, and if we would learn to sing with them, they can also teach us the values of the new Jerusalem.

## Focusing Attention

That which claims our deepest attention makes us what we are. If we concentrate upon what happens around us and become absorbed with the affairs of men and nations, we inevitably become cynical and disillusioned with life. If we turn inward and direct attention upon ourselves, we shrivel in our own little sphere of experience, ultimately becoming enslaved to the dying flesh. But if we focus attention upon God and the greatness of His Being, seeking to interpret all that is in the light of His Word, then our minds and spirits pulsate with the heartbeat of the universe, and existence takes on deathless, joyous meaning.

Of course we notice what commands our interest. I am re-

LXXI (1952): pp. 75–84; J. J. O'Rourke, "The Hymns of the Apocalypse" *Catholic Biblical Quarterly* XXX (1968): 399–409; E. F. Siegman, "Apocalypse," *New Catholic Encyclopedia* I (New York: McGraw-Hill, 1967), p. 659; and Evelyn Underhill, *Worship* (New York: Harper & Row, 1957), pp. 91–93.

[10] Quoted by L. E. Maxwell, in "Perspective," *The Prairie Overcomer*, February 1978, p. 91.

minded of a boy who went up on Lookout Mountain, a nearby peak famous for its beautiful panoramic view of seven states. It was a clear day, and he could see thirty miles in every direction; the scenic landscape was decked in brilliant autumn foliage. Asked later what he observed, the boy replied: "It's the first time I ever saw the backside of a buzzard, and him a-flying." How like people, in perceiving the Presence of God! With His infinite glory in our midst and the limitless vistas of His kingdom on every side, often all we notice is a buzzard.

Doubtless this is one reason many persons today have no sense of stability amid the constant turmoil of the world. Since they have only a feeble apprehension of the everlasting God, temporal concerns of the moment have crowded out the celestial dimension of life. Little wonder there is no spring in their steps, no shout in their souls. If we are to overcome the listlessness and despair of this age, then we must get our eyes off the fluctuating waves of time and fix them on the tide of God's eternal purpose.[11]

## Truth for Hard Times

The Revelation is written by John[12] in the form of a letter to the seven churches of Asia (1:4,11). These congregations, described in Revelation 2 and 3, typify the church at large. They exhibit in their spiritual life many of the same conditions—from warm, evangelical devotion to apathetic lovelessness and apostasy—that may be found in churches today.

---

[11] My analogy is taken from a letter General William Booth, of the Salvation Army, wrote to his daughter at a time when she was discouraged, advising her to keep her eyes off the waves and fix them on the tide. Told by Arthur Wallis, *In The Day of Thy Power* (London: Christian Literature Crusade, 1956), p. 204.

[12] Though the text simply identifies the author as John (1:1,4,9; 22:8), it is generally believed that he is the "beloved disciple," the apostle John, who wrote the Gospel and letters that bear his name. I see no good reason why this would not be the case.

Significantly, after each fellowship is addressed, there comes
the command, "hear what the Spirit says to the churches." It
is a present appeal, emphasizing that the truths are applicable to the church of John's day, as well as in every succeeding
generation.

For those believers who first read the letter, it was a time
of extreme adversity in the world. The totalitarian Roman
government under which they lived was oppressive and, in
many areas, openly hostile. Christians often were singled out
for scorn and punishment because of their refusal to observe
the idolatrous practices of Roman pagan culture, and many
were killed for their faith. Under the mad decrees of Nero in
A.D. 67, multitudes went through unspeakable tortures. Some
were fed to lions in public arenas, for the amusement of
gawking spectators; some were sewed up in skins and then
molested by wild dogs until they expired; some were saturated with oil, nailed to crosses in the emperor's gardens, and
then burned alive. Amid this persecution, both Paul and
Peter were martyred. When the Revelation was written,
probably about A.D. 95–97,[13] the church was being subjected
to another reign of terror under Domitian's rule, in which no
less than 40,000 Christians were slain. During this period,
Timothy, the bishop of Ephesus, was beaten to death by an
enraged mob, and John himself was banished to the Isle of
Patmos for his witness (1:9).[14]

------

[13] Some authorities have placed the time of writing as early as the
reign of Nero, but the later date seems more probable. There is no evidence that Nero banished men to exile, and also, it hardly seems likely
that the development of the churches in Asia would have been very far
along by the seventh decade of the century.

[14] According to Irenaeus, one of the early church fathers, John was ar-
rested at the time of Domitian's persecution and sentenced to work in
the mines on this rocky island in the Aegean Sea, where a government
penal colony was maintained. For more detailed information about these
early oppressions of the church, *see* Thieleman J. van Braght, comp., *The
Bloody Theater or Martyrs' Mirror of the Defenseless Christians* (Scott-
dale, PA: Herald Press, © 1950), pp. 1–99; or a less extensive account in

Here in exile from family and friends, bent from long hours of forced labor, the aged apostle, now in his eighties, sends this message to encourage and comfort those whose faith is being sorely tried. It would be reassuring for them to know that the tribulations through which the church passes are not the last word, and that God is still in control.

But more deadly than the oppression of a hostile world is the enemy lurking within the church. The beleaguered Christians faced constant pressure to give up their witness, or at least work out an accommodation with the sensate culture about them. For some believers already enslaved by this temptation, the letter comes as an appeal for repentance, renewal, and holy living. For all Christians, it is a prophetic summons to vigilance against the deceptiveness of Satan, by making sure that Christ is indeed Lord of our lives.

A special blessing is promised to all who read, hear, and heed what is written in the book (1:3; 22:7). The injunction at the beginning and end is associated with the imminence of Christ's coming, which accentuates the urgency of the message. Clearly, the momentous truth of Revelation is not to be taken lightly.

## Ways of Interpretation

How to understand the time frame of the events and persons described is another matter. Generally there is no problem with the opening section of the book, where at least some of the things prophesied would be fulfilled in the near future (1:1,3). But when we move beyond chapter 3, the interpretation of chronology and historical information becomes more difficult. Because different conclusions are possible, honesty, if not modesty, should keep us from dogmatizing our own opinions.

---

William Bryon Torbush, *Foxe's Book of Martyrs* (Philadelphia: John C. Winston Co., 1926). A good picture of Domitian and his pretentious reign is in Ethelbert Stauffer, *Christ and the Caesars* (London: SCM Press, 1955), pp. 147–191.

Basically, views fall into four categories, though combinations are possible. Preterists see the book as depicting events of the first century, when the church was engaged in a mortal struggle with the Roman Empire. The conflict is viewed by historicists as a general forecast of the whole course of church history, from John's day up to the end of the world. Futurists locate the major portion of the book in the events surrounding the Lord's Second Coming. Then there are those who entirely spiritualize the Revelation, separating its imagery from history, in an effort to find universal principles, applicable in any age.[15] Entering into the interpretation of the book, too, is one's understanding of the millennium (20:1–10): whether the promised reign of blessedness is symbolical of the church age or is a literal period of time on this earth, prior to or following the Second Advent of Christ.

These views reflect upon the way the book's content may be arranged in outline. Needless to say, there is no end to variations. But however arranged, the songs, insofar as they are lifted up to God, transcend time and space and constitute an epic of their own. They are the primary unifying element in the narrative, as the church militant on earth (1:1–3:22) moves through struggle and martyrdom (4:1–20:15) to become the church triumphant in heaven (21:1–22:17).

## Style of Writing

The rich imagery and symbolism in which the Revelation is cast adds to its wonder. Like the exaggerated figures often seen in mural art, as well as in political cartoons, it depicts truth in bold, imaginative pictures, rather than in systematic

---

[15] An elaboration of these positions is not essential to our study, but, if one would like to explore the subject further, general presentations may be found in almost any commentary. Summary statements also will be noted in Merrill C. Tenney, op. cit., pp. 135–146; Kenneth A. Strand, *Interpreting the Book of Revelations* (Ann Arbor: Ann Arbor Publishers, 1976), pp. 11–16; and William Graham Scroggie, *The Great Unveiling* (Edinburgh: the Author, 1920); among others.

logic. Such language is especially appropriate to the visions that the book describes.[16] Dramatic descriptions, like the sacraments, assist the mind in visualizing and feeling the deep spiritual dimensions of reality. Without in any way depreciating its authenticity, the style makes truth more vivid to the senses.

This form of writing was quite common in the ancient world, especially in apocalyptic literature. It was a sort of sign language. The cryptic phrases, numbers, sounds, and colors, as well as the often rather bizarre-looking creatures and actions, conveyed hidden meanings easily perceived by the code community but largely unintelligible to those without. For this reason, it was well suited to oppressed people who desired a protected form of communication. The Judeo-Christian community had an apocalyptic parlance of its own, into which this letter fit.[17] But by far the most informative reference was the sacred Scripture—that body of inerrant truth cherished within the church. Persons familiar with this teaching would have little difficulty understanding Revelation.

No other inspired book from the first century is so saturated with the thought forms of the Old Testament. B. F. Westcott and F. J. A. Hort estimate that of the 404 verses in

---

[16] The Revelation comes to John in the form of visions, as he is caught up in the Spirit. Altogether, words that refer to perception by sight, such as "I saw" or "behold," occur 140 times in the book.

[17] If one is interested in learning about this type of literature, which flourished between 200 B.C. and A.D. 100, see Frank Chamberlin Porter, *The Messages of the Apocalyptic Writers* (London: James Clark, 1914); F. Crawford Burkitt, *Jewish and Christian Apocalypses* (London: Oxford University, 1914); and R. H. Charles, *Religious Development Between the Old and New Testaments* (London: Williams & Norgate, 1927). A more recent work which bears upon this study, especially in the composition of John's Apocalypse, is Austin Farrer's, *A Rebirth of Images* (Boston: Beacon Press, 1949). Though concerned with the larger subject of image communication, it presents some interesting insights to the Jewish-Christian mind of the first century.

Revelation, 265 contain references to the Jewish Bible, and
that approximately 550 passages in the Old Testament are
involved.[18] Concepts out of Daniel, Isaiah, Ezekiel, Zechariah, and the Psalms seem most prominent. There are also
numerous parallels in the Revelation to the teachings of
Jesus, particularly His Olivet discourse (Matt. 24:3-25:46).
From the standpoint of using Scripture to explain Scripture,
the Apocalypse is surely the capstone of the Bible. In a fitting
sense, it gathers all the great themes of Holy Writ and brings
them to awesome fulfillment before the throne of God.

## Plan of This Study

We shall seek, in the next pages, to lift out the songs in the
Revelation, see them in their context, analyze their essential
messages, and then apply some pertinent aspects of the truth
to our lives today. In keeping with the theme, scattered
throughout the book are selected stanzas from some hymns
still sung in the church.

The book has grown out of my own devotional study, as I
have sought to learn more of the meaning of worship, and, in
turn, to lead a small group of students in this same quest. It is
intended for meditative reading and reflection, not academic
disputation. However, extensive research has gone into its
preparation, particularly in examining the original Greek
text and consulting scholarly commentaries from a variety of
perspectives.[19] A good deal of background probing also has

---

[18] B. F. Westcott and F. J. A. Hort, *The New Testament In the Original
Greek* (New York: Harper & Brothers, 1882), pp. 184-188. Ronald H.
Preston and Anthony T. Hanson count 518 Old Testament references.
*The Revelation of St. John the Divine* (London: SCM Press, 1949), p. 24.
The latter work also has an excellent statement on the way John uses the
Old Testament, pp. 34-42.

[19] If I were to single out a work, I think Robert H. Mounce's, *The Book
of Revelation*, New International Commentary (Grand Rapids: Wm. B.
Eerdmans, 1977), has been most appreciated. Its objective treatment of
the text and its wide acquaintance with the significant literature in the

been done in areas of specialized interest. The footnotes may prove helpful for those who want to explore the subject more fully.

To get the most from the book, let me suggest that you try to bring the songs into your own quiet moments of prayer. As an aid in your meditation, you might want to memorize the songs, using your favorite translation. Then turn them over in your mind when you wait before the throne, and, as it were, sing along with the choirs of heaven. I know of no more uplifting exercise to the soul. After all, these hymns are sung in the Presence of the King, and we have every right to join the celebration.

So, for a little while, lay aside the pressing cares of this age, shut out the screeching noise of a passing world, and fix your

---

field make the book a very useful reference. For exegesis of the Greek, Henry Barclay Swete's, *The Apocalypse of St. John* (London: Macmillan, 1909) is outstanding; as well as James Moffatt's, *The Revelation of St. John* V, Expositor's Greek Testament (Grand Rapids: Wm. B. Eerdmans, 1961 © 1910). The two-volume work of R. H. Charles, *The Revelation of St. John*, International Critical Commentary (Edinburgh: T & T Clark, 1920), also leans heavily on the Greek and is especially helpful in comparing the text with relevant apocalyptic literature. Less comprehensive, but providing a wealth of historical and linguistic information, is G. B. Caird, *A Commentary on the Revelation of St. John the Divine*, New Testament Commentaries (New York: Harper & Row, 1966). For sheer exposition, especially on practical application, Joseph S. Exell, *Revelation*, The Biblical Illustrator (Grand Rapids: Baker Book House, 1963), offers many insights. Other commentators who have been useful in my study include Leon Morris, George R. Beasley-Murray, Joseph Augustus Seiss, A. S. Peake, Walter Scott, Martin Kiddle, Jonathan Edwards, William Milligan, Ray Summers, R. C. H. Lenski, William Hendriksen, A. B. Simpson, G. Campbell Morgan, Herschel H. Hobbs, Ray Frank Robbins, Hanns Lilje, William Barclay, John Walvoord, George Eldon Ladd, William R. Newell, R. H. Preston, A. K. Hanson, A. J. Gordon, Martin H. Franzmann, Austin Farrer, Michael Wilcock, Mathias Rissi, Apostolos Makrakis, Donald Grey Barnhouse, and Thomas F. Torrance. A good bibliography of generally accessible materials on Revelation may be found in Mounce, op. cit., pp. 49–60.

attention upon those realities that are eternal. Behold the Lord in His glory! Though our vision may be dim, someday the clouds will be rolled away, and we shall see Him as He is. The songs that we have sung now, in His Word, we shall sing then, in His Presence.

Peter Bohler once said to Charles Wesley, "If I had a thousand tongues, I'd praise Christ with all of them." Wesley was so impressed by this statement that, approaching the first anniversary of his conversion, on May 21, 1739, he wrote that matchless hymn, "O For a Thousand Tongues to Sing My Great Redeemer's Praise." It expresses well the feeling that has grown in my soul during the writing of these devotional studies. If they can help another sense more of this same longing, my purpose in their preparation will have been fulfilled.

O for a thousand tongues to sing
    My great Redeemer's praise,
The glories of my God and King,
    The triumphs of his grace!

My gracious Master and my God,
    Assist me to proclaim,
To spread through all the earth abroad
    The honors of thy name.

Jesus! the name that charms our fears,
    That bids our sorrows cease,
'Tis music in the sinners' ears,
    'Tis life, and health, and peace.

He breaks the power of canceled sin,
    He sets the prisoner free;
His blood can make the foulest clean;
    His blood availed for me.

He speaks, and listening to his voice,
New life the dead receive;
The mournful, broken hearts rejoice;
The humble poor, believe.

Hear him, ye deaf; his praise, ye dumb,
Your loosened tongues employ;
Ye blind, behold your Savior come;
And leap, ye lame, for joy.

CHARLES WESLEY

# 1

# *The Anthem of the Triune God*

"Holy, holy, holy, is the Lord God, the Almighty,
who was and who is and who is to come."

REVELATION 4:8

## Guardians of the Throne

The throne of Caesar appeared as the center of all authority in the Roman world. But to some inhabitants of that world who were more discerning, there was another throne—a throne established high above the earth—and He who sat upon it ruled over all.

It is here, after describing conditions in the church, that the Revelation pauses to gain perspective, before showing the judgments to come (4:1,2). Portrayed in rich apocalyptic imagery, the seated King has the appearance of a jasper stone, probably a diamond, and a ruby-red sardius. These precious stones in their brilliance speak of God's glory and purity, on the one hand, and His justice and redemptive plan, on the other (4:3; cf., 21:11).[1] Adding to the dazzl-

---

[1] The sardius, or carnelian, is the first stone in the breastplate of the Old Testament high priests, and the jasper is the last (*see* Ex. 28:17). Probably the mention of these particular stones is intended to include those in between, and since each tribe of Israel is represented by a stone, it is a symbolic way of bringing the chosen people of God into the throne scene. Significantly, too, the jasper is the first stone in the foundation and walls of the city of God (21:18,19); while the sardius also appears in the foundations of the new Jerusalem (21:20).

ing brightness of His Presence, while still showing restraint in depicting detail, is an emerald-green rainbow that encircles the throne (4:3). Perhaps it is a reference to the bow seen in Ezekiel's vision of the glory of the Lord (Ezk. 1:28), though more likely it is reminiscent of God's covenant with His people after the Flood (Gen. 9:12–17). It is a symbol of living hope in the midst of judgment, and assurance of grace to those who keep His Word. God is faithful who has promised.

Out of the throne come flashes of lightning and sounds and peals of thunder, expressive of the Presence and power of the Almighty (4:5; 8:5; 11:19; 16:18). A similar manifestation accompanies the appearance of God at the giving of the Law at Sinai (Ex. 19:16) and thereafter comes to represent omnipotence in speaking (e.g., Job 37:4,5; Psa. 77:18; Ezk. 1:13).

Continually burning before the throne are seven torches of fire, which are the seven spirits of God (4:5). The number *seven* underscores completeness,[2] thus symbolizing here the perfect operation of the Holy Spirit in His fullness (cf., 1:4; 3:1; 5:6). The figure may be taken from Isaiah 11:2, which speaks of seven modes of the Spirit's manifestation, or perhaps the seven-branched lampstand in the temple (Ex. 25:31, 32; 2 Chron. 4:2–6). Fire, as a symbol of the Spirit, accents His illuminating and purifying activity. God is a consuming flame.

Intensifying this scene of absolute holiness in front of the

---

[2] Seven enters largely into the plan of the whole book. There are seven letters to the seven churches, seven candlesticks, seven angels, seven spirits, seven seals, seven trumpets, seven vials, seven stars in Christ's right hand, seven horns and seven eyes of the Lamb, seven lamps, seven thunders, a dragon with seven heads and seven crowns, seven mountains, seven kings, and so forth. This number is conspicuous throughout the Bible. For example: God rested in creation on the seventh day; every seventh year was a sabbatical; every seventh sabbatical year was a jubilee; there were seven weeks between Passover and Pentecost; at Passover service, seven lambs were offered daily—to mention only a few. Symbolically, seven points to completeness, totality, fullness, and perfection.

throne is what seems to be a sea of glass, clear as crystal (4:6). The vast expanse of crystalline sea, mirroring on its surface the many colored lights shining from the throne, forms a barrier to the Presence of God. He who dwells in unapproachable light is seen as utterly transcendent and separate from that which He has made.

In the center, round about the throne and constituting an inner circle, are four living creatures (4:6–8).[3] These mystical beings are "full of eyes in front and behind," depicting an all-seeing position of watchfulness toward God and His creation. Nothing is hidden from their sight. They have six wings, signifying the swiftness by which they can execute the will of God. Each has a different form: one like a lion, one like an ox, one with the face of a man, and one like a flying eagle. These were emblems that appeared in the banners of the four nearest tribes assembled around the tabernacle in the wilderness, suggesting an association with God's chosen people. In a wider sense, the four forms of life picture "whatever is noblest, strongest, wisest and swiftest in animate nature,"[4] and hence manifest the highest in creaturehood before the throne. That there are four of them, a number that recalls the four points of the compass, suggests their representation of the whole created cosmos.

---

[3] The description of these heavenly beings as "beasts" in the King James Version is unfortunate. I note that the New King James Bible changes the translation to "living creatures," which is a much better rendering of the term. Later in Revelation, a word is properly translated *beast* (e.g., 13:1), but it is not the same term used in reference to these creatures about the throne.

[4] H. B. Swete, *The Apocalypse of St. John* (London: Macmillan, 1909), p. 71. This is by no means the only interpretation that can be given to these creatures. Another appealing view, though less likely, is that they represent four attributes of God in His care of creation. By this theory, the characteristics of bravery, strength, intelligence, and speed seen in these forms of life symbolize aspects of divine vigilance. Still less support can be found for the view that they reflect four aspects of Christ's ministry.

Elsewhere in Scripture, these exalted beings are probably
the seraphim and cherubim described in visions of the throne
(Isa. 6:1–4; Ezk. 1:4–21).[5] As guardians of the throne, they
live in the immediate Presence of God. Their domain is
beautifully depicted in the furnishings of the tabernacle,
where the curtains forming the interior of the tent were in-
woven with cherubic figures (Ex. 26:1,31). Also, above the
Ark of the Covenant, the physical symbol of God's heavenly
throne, two cherubim were sculptured, facing each other,
with their outstretched wings enfolding the Mercy Seat (Ex.
25:17–22). In the temple constructed by Solomon, the same
imagery, on a larger scale, abounded (1 Kings 6:23–29). There
"between the two cherubim" God dwelt (Num. 7:89; cf. Psa.
80:1; Psa. 99:1; 1 Sam. 4:4; 2 Sam. 6:2; Isa. 37:16).

In special ways, these throne attendants serve as God's
ministers of righteousness. Cherubim with flaming swords
were stationed at the entrance of Eden, to defend it from un-
hallowed intrusion by fallen creatures, while also symbolically protecting the garden for man's future occupancy (Gen.
3:24). In Ezekiel, the cherubim are seen actively administering judgment upon rebellious Israel by taking fire and hand-
ing it to an angel, to cast upon Jerusalem (Ezk. 10:7; cf., Ezk.
10:1–22). Isaiah gives a similar picture, of a seraph taking a
live coal off the altar with tongs and placing it upon the unclean lips of the prophet, to cleanse him from sin (Isa. 6:6,7).
Living so near to God, these heavenly beings understood full

---

[5] Whether these beings are identical or separate forms of angelic life is
unclear. The seraphim, meaning "burning ones," are only mentioned by
Isaiah; while the cherubim, or cherub in the singular, are mentioned
about ninety times in Scripture. Whatever the relationship, both manifest a flaming zeal for the worship and service of God. For more information, see Herbert Lockyer, *The Mystery and Ministry of Angels*
(Grand Rapids: Wm. B. Eerdmans, 1958), pp. 23–28; or Patrick Fair-
bairn's exhaustive treatment in *The Typology of Scripture* (Edinburgh: T
& T Clark, 1870), pp. 259–286.

well that without holiness, no one may enter into His Presence.

The love and zeal of these beings can be seen supremely in their worship. John says that "day and night they do not cease" to lift their voices in praise to God (4:8). In this constancy of adoration, we see the preeminent quality of life associated with "the living creatures"—life as it is, or shall be, for those who live closest to the throne of the Most High.

## The Nature of God

"Holy, holy, holy, is the Lord God, the Almighty, who was and who is and who is to come," they sing (4:8). The threefold affirmation suggests the Trinity of Persons in the Godhead, all of whom share equally in the divine attributes.[6] It is very similar to the trisagion of the seraphim in Isaiah 6:3: "Holy, Holy, Holy, is the Lord of hosts."

Holiness, in a profound sense, is the quality most basic to the essential nature of God. The word *holiness* comes from a root meaning "separateness" or "apartness," indicating in reference to God that He is self-existent and independent from all other beings. Not only is God separate from any law or power external to Himself, but He is also utterly undefiled by any iniquity within His nature. He is of purer eyes than to approve evil (Hab. 1:13). God cannot countenance even the thought of sin (Heb. 7:26). In the integrity of His character, it is impossible for Him to act otherwise than in accordance with absolute perfection, for all that He wills is holy.

The praise of the Holy One leads to the acknowledgment of His sovereignty. God is the Lord over all, the Almighty. He can do whatever He pleases (Psa. 115:3). He has made the heavens and the earth by His mighty power and outstretched arm! Nothing is too difficult for Him (Jer. 32:17). All the re-

---

[6] The number three often relates to the divine nature in Scripture. In this song, the number is compounded by the succession of three phrases, each with three descriptions of God, forming a perfect trisagion.

sources of the universe are at His command. Nations before Him "are like a drop from a bucket, And are regarded as a speck of dust on the scales" (Isa. 40:15). "He it is who reduces rulers to nothing, Who makes the judges of the earth meaningless" (Isa. 40:23). With just a word, God can strike every creature to the ground. "It is I who put to death and give life," He says. "I have wounded, and it is I who heal; And there is no one who can deliver from My hand" (Deut. 32:39).

Completing the trilogy, God, who is holy and omnipotent, is also eternal: He "was, and is, and is to come." This phrase of the song reflects God's naming of Himself to Moses: "I am who I am" (Ex. 3:14). He stands above time, free from all temporal distinctions. In His Being there is no succession, no beginning or ending, no past or future—all is present in Him. Time itself is of His making. The works of man "will become old as a garment," but God is "the same" (Heb. 1:11,12). With Him there is "no variation, or shifting shadow" (James 1:17).

## Only God Is Great

The song immediately brings one to contemplate the essence of the divine nature. His Being is the foundation for all His deeds. So before telling us what He does, the heavenly creatures tell us who He is.

Significantly, it is the holiness of God that is first emphasized. Listening to the chatter of our experience-centered culture today, we might have thought that the singers would start with love. But then, the songs of our day seldom reflect the priorities of heaven. Certainly God is love, but it is holy love, a love always in unmitigated opposition to evil. Such love wants only the best for its beloved, and the best God knows is Himself. So He says, "You shall be holy, for I am holy" (1 Peter 1:16). By giving preeminence to this quality of life, the initial song declares God's design for all His creatures, while also showing that perfect love can only be satisfied when its object is holy.

We need to capture afresh this heavenly perspective. It will bring a new sense of realism and humility into our lives, even as it did for the prophet Isaiah, when he saw the Lord on His throne, high and lifted up (Isa. 6:1–8). Before the pure otherness of a thrice-holy God, unclean man is made to tremble. If seraphim were so overwhelmed at the sight that they covered their eyes and feet (a way of expressing reverential awe and deep humility), then it is not surprising that mortal man feels undone in the presence of the Shechinah glory. A vision of holiness shows us how far short we have come from the divine image and invokes honest confession of our impurity, with resultant cleansing by the blood.

Absolute sovereignty also is a note sadly missing in the pronouncements of this world. Man likes to think that he is self-sufficient, or at least God's little helper. It is a blow to human pride, to acknowledge that the Almighty needs nothing from man to complete His perfection.[7] Even the scenes of heaven's joy are not for God's benefit, as if He lacked something in Himself; the songs are but expressions of His creatures' submission. The singing is not by God, but in front of Him. God is His own existence. He is His own reason. He is His own cause. He is His own activity. He is above every compulsion, every desire, every fate.

To weary pilgrims feeling the oppression of swaggering world tyrants in that first century, no less than in ours, this

---

[7] What is affirmed in these songs stands in antithesis to all other religions of biblical times, which, in effect, made God a convenience to man's selfish desires. Cultic religions invariably are designed for the creature to get his own way, seeking, through man-directed techniques, to manipulate God. The serious student who would like a penetrating analysis from the standpoint of the Old Testament should read Yehezk El Kaufmann, *The Religion of Israel*, trans. Moshe Greenberg (Chicago: University of Chicago Press, 1960), pp. 1–149.

truth brought welcome reassurance to the soul. God is long-suffering, but He is never limited by any weakness, when He wants to act. That is why His will shall be done on earth, as it is done in heaven.

Even more, His nature will never change. God is forever the same, "from everlasting to everlasting" (Psa. 90:2). A generation bewildered by constant upheaval, one that weighs values in terms of current fads, may have difficulty comprehending the timeful-ness of the eternal present, but this quality of God causes ceaseless praise among the hosts of heaven. Herein is our joy, amid the ebb and flow of the passing world: Our God remains unmoved, and His throne endures forever.

At the funeral of Louis XIV, the priest looked down at the casket containing the body of the once-powerful monarch of France, with the luxurious robes of royalty concealing the cold form within. Then, turning to the assembled nobility present, he began his oration: "My friends, only God is great!"

Indeed, this truth should be obvious to all. But if it is not realized on this earth, we may be sure that it is proclaimed in heaven, and to Him alone every knee shall bow, "and every tongue shall give praise to God" (Rom. 14:11; cf., Isa. 45:22,23).

Holy, holy, holy! Lord God Almighty!
Early in the morning our song shall rise to thee;
Holy, holy, holy! merciful and mighty;
God in three persons, blessed Trinity!

Holy, holy, holy! All the saints adore thee,
Casting down their golden crowns around the glassy sea;
Cherubim and seraphim falling down before thee,
Which wert, and art, and evermore shalt be.

Holy, holy, holy! Though the darkness hide thee,
Though the eye of sinful man thy glory may not see;

Only thou art holy; there is none beside thee,
Perfect in power, in love, and purity.

Holy, holy, holy! Lord God Almighty!
All thy works shall praise thy name in earth and sky and sea;
Holy, holy, holy! merciful and mighty;
God in three persons, blessed Trinity!

REGINALD HEBER

# 2

# *The Creation Hymn*

"Worthy art Thou, our Lord and our God,
to receive glory and honor and power; for
Thou didst create all things, and because
of Thy will they existed, and were created."

REVELATION 4:11

## The Twenty-four Elders

A young musician was being congratulated by admiring
friends after his first public recital in a concert hall. One man
said to him, "Your music truly lifted my soul, but I am curi-
ous to know why you kept your eyes turned toward the second balcony."

The violinist replied, "My master was up there, and when I
saw the smile on his face, I knew that he was pleased."

Perhaps that is why the heavenly hosts keep their eyes
turned toward Him who sits on the throne. They want to see
the smile on His face, as they offer all their gifts unto Him
who is worthy.

As the most exalted of the created beings give to Him
glory, honor, and thanks (4:9), the twenty-four elders join the
adoration. Pictured as seated on twenty-four thrones surrounding the central throne of God, they are clothed in white
raiment, and on their heads are crowns of gold (4:4).

Whether glorified saints or some form of angelic creation, this holy order represents the people of God before
the throne. There may be a parallel to the elders, sometimes
translated "ancients," which Isaiah mentions as a heavenly

council, reigning with the Lord of hosts (Isa. 24:23). In their earthly prototype, they reflect the twenty-four courses of priests who continually served before the altar (1 Chron. 24:5–18) and the twenty-four courses of Levites always on duty in the temple, to praise God with cymbals, psalters, and harps (1 Chron. 25:6–31). That they are twenty-four elders, doubling the number twelve that is associated with divine government, incorporates the twelve tribes of Israel and the twelve apostles of the Lamb, thus uniting the people of the old and the new covenant.[1] Their white robes and golden crowns, emblems of regal character, further identify them with those who are triumphant in Christ and reign with Him in glory (cf., 1:6; 2:10; 3:14,21; Luke 22:30; Matt. 19:27,28).[2]

Yet the picture of the elders does not end with them seated on their thrones as royal counselors of God. As the majestic song of the living creatures swells through the courts of heaven, the elders "fall down before Him who sits on the throne, and will worship Him who lives forever and ever" (4:10).[3] So great is their sense of the numinous that, in a gesture of grateful homage, they take from their brows the golden crowns and cast them before the feet of God.

---

[1] These two groups are clearly joined in the description of the new Jerusalem, when the names of the twelve patriarchs are inscribed on the twelve gates and the names of the twelve apostles are written on the foundations of the wall (21:12,14).

[2] For a more complete treatment of the elders, see G. H. Lang, *The Revelation of Jesus Christ* (London: Paternoster Press, 1945), pp. 124–136; and N. B. Stonehouse, "The Elders and the Living Beings in the Apocalypse," *Paul Before the Areopagus* (Grand Rapids: Wm. B. Eerdmans, 1957), pp. 88–108.

[3] In the New Testament, falling down, as an intentional act, is usually joined to worship. It is a way of intensifying the sense of obeisance to God. Interestingly, the word for *worship* originally conveyed the idea of placing oneself in a lowly position, to kiss the feet of deity, and hence to bow down or to prostrate oneself. Gerhard Kittel and Gerhard Friedrich, eds., *Theological Dictionary of the New Testament* VI (Grand Rapids: Wm. B. Eerdmans, 1969), p. 163.

These crowns beautifully typify the honor conferred by God upon His people for their faithful service (2:10; 2 Tim. 4:8; James 1:12; 1 Peter 5:4; 1 Cor. 9:25),[4] while the gold, a precious metal symbolic of the divine character, suggests the quality of life that they have received in Christ. All the dross, the impurity, is gone, burned away in the refining fires of holiness, so that only the pure gold—that which is godlike in nature—remains, to form the substance of their victory garland. Yet, as the reward of their labor presses upon their brow, the elders know that every good thing they have comes through no merit of their own; it is all a gift of God. And in recognition of His worthiness, totally submissive to His will, they remove their golden crowns and lay them before the throne of their Lord.

## The Creator's Praise

As they return to God that which He has given, the elders lift their hearts in praise, saying, "Worthy art Thou, our Lord and our God, to receive glory and honor and power; for Thou didst create all things, and because of Thy will they existed, and were created" (4:11).

The hymn affirms the incomparable worthiness of their Lord and God. At the same time, it is a clear rejection of the self-acclaimed deity of the Emperor Domitian, whose entrance in triumphant procession would be greeted with the words, "Worthy art thou," while his devotees in the popular cult of emperor worship addressed him as "our Lord and God."[5] It was because the Christians refused to confess the

---

[4] The word for *crown* here designates a wreath given as a prize for victory, achievement, or personal merit, as distinguished from the word denoting a king's diadem. For an exhaustive treatment of both terms, *see* ibid. VII, 1970, pp. 615–636.

[5] Hanns Lilje, *The Last Book of the Bible*, trans. Olive Wyon (Philadelphia: Muhlenberg Press, 1957), pp. 108, 109; cf. Ethelbert Stauffer, *Christ and the Caesars* (London: SCM Press, 1955), pp. 150–159.

arrogant claims of Caesar that many of them were tortured and killed. By ascribing glory, honor, and power to Him who sits on the throne of heaven, the church was saying that it would have no part in the idolatrous religion of this world, nor could it ever be so foolish as to worship a debased creature of the dust.

Only He is worthy who has created the universe, He by whose will all things exist and have their being. The song sees creation formed in the mind of God before the worlds were made and the stars fixed in place. What a masterful way to humble man! We are reminded that creation would not even have been called into being, apart from God's sovereign pleasure.

But what about the presence of evil in the world? If everything comes from God, what responsibility does the creature have for humanity's woes? Or is there an ultimate dualism in the universe, with some kind of evil power coexisting with God?

To these deep questions, the song speaks in eloquent simplicity. Yes, prior to creation there was nothing but God, so all that is has its existence in Him alone, including the aboriginal form of Satan and his cohorts. However, the holiness of God precludes any possibility of evil in His handiwork. Depravity, whatever its embodiment, is the willful corruption of that which God has created holy.

Seen in the light of the throne, as the elders behold their sovereign Lord, all that is made is recognized, in its beginning, as an external expression of God's perfection, a display of His own internal glory and fullness. "The heavens are telling of the glory of God; And their expanse is declaring the work of His hands" (Psa. 19:1). When God looked upon it, He pronounced it "very good" (Gen. 1:31). Nevertheless, creation is not a part of God's essence, an extension of His deity, since He is complete in Himself. That which He has made unmistakenly bears the mark of its Creator, of which man is the supreme image, but creation in any form is still separate from God and is never to be worshiped. Only the sovereign Architect and Builder is worthy of honor.

## The Human Response

Man's fulfillment comes in knowing God's glory, loving Him for it, and rejoicing in it, and in this exercise consists God's honor and praise. That is, in acknowledging the glory of God, the creature experiences the happiness for which he was made, while exhibiting to God the excellency of His own work, wherein He is pleased. It is all of God. To use Jonathan Edwards's analogy of sunlight, the beams of glory came from God and are returned to Him; "the refulgence shines upon and into the creature, and is reflected back to the luminary."[6] As Charles Wesley sang:

> O all-creating God,
>     At whose supreme decree
> My body rose, a breathing clod—
>     My soul sprang forth from Thee.
>
> For this Thou has design'd,
>     And form'd me man for this—
> To know and love Thyself, and find
>     In Thee my endless bliss.

Herein is the purpose of creation. In the familiar words of the shorter catechism, "Man's chief end is to glorify God, and to enjoy Him forever."[7] Whenever this end is reversed and man's primary quest becomes his own glory, then God's will

---

[6] Jonathan Edwards, "Dissertation Concerning the End for Which God Created the World," *Works of President Edwards* II (Leavitt and Allen, 1858), p. 255. The ambitious student who does not mind laborious reading will be abundantly rewarded in working through this whole dissertation.

[7] The Westminster Shorter Catechism, *The Confession of Faith* (Richmond: John Knox Press, 1964), p. 391.

is perverted, and sin comes into being.[8] In this distortion, the creature assumes the role of the Creator, and the glory of the incorruptible God is changed into a lie (Rom. 1:18–32). How this happens is illustrated in the worship of Caesar and the sensual glorification of the flesh in the Roman world. But just as perilously, it can be seen in the self-indulging, pleasure-oriented life-style of our generation. We may have more refined ways of asserting our independence, but the principle of creature deification is no less real.

The white-clad elders, offering all they are and all they have to God, set before us a better example. It is a submission free, yet unreserved, and in its devotion there is a peace that fills the heart with joy and life with praise.

General William Booth, of the Salvation Army, was once asked to reveal the secret of his success. The devout leader hesitated a moment, then, as tears came into his eyes and ran down his face, he replied: "I will tell you the secret. God has had all there was of me to have. There may have been men with greater opportunities; but from the day I got the poor of London on my heart, and a vision of what Jesus Christ could do, I made up my mind that God would have all there was of William Booth. If there is anything of power in the Salvation Army today, it is because God has had all the adoration of my heart, all the power of my will, and all the influence of my life."[9]

---

[8] One of the most provocative and influential treatments of this subject that I have seen is Jonathan Edwards's, "The Nature of True Virtue," *Works*, op. cit., pp. 261–308. In this work he shows that to be good, one must treat everything according to its true worth. This pertains to God as purest Being, as well as to His creation, including man. Thus, by this reasoning, to treat God like a man or, adversely, to give man the place of God, violates the nature of virtue and thereby causes sin.

[9] Taken from a reported conversation of Wilbur Chapman, famous Presbyterian evangelist, with General Booth, which I saw printed in a local church-news bulletin. Though I have been unable to find a published primary source, several Salvation Army leaders with whom I have talked have verified the substantial accuracy of the quotation.

Would that this could be said of all of us. Here, finally, is our only reasonable response to the revelation of Him who sits upon the throne. Whatever our calling might be, God deserves all the adoration of our hearts, all the power of our wills, and all the influence of our lives.

> Come, almighty to deliver,
> Let us all Thy life receive;
> Suddenly return, and never,
> Nevermore Thy temples leave.
> Thee we would be always blessing,
> Serve Thee as Thy hosts above,
> Pray and praise Thee without ceasing,
> Glory in Thy perfect love.
>
> Finish then Thy new creation,
> Pure and spotless let us be;
> Let us see Thy great salvation
> Perfectly restored in Thee:
> Changed from glory into glory,
> Till in heaven we take our place,
> Till we cast our crowns before Thee,
> Lost in wonder, love and praise.

CHARLES WESLEY

# 3

# *The New Song of Redemption*

"Worthy art Thou to take the book, and to break its seals; for Thou wast slain, and didst purchase for God with Thy blood men from every tribe and tongue and people and nation. And Thou has made them to be a kingdom and priests to our God; and they will reign upon the earth."

REVELATION 5:9,10

### The Destiny of Creation

The ancient Greeks told of an art contest in which the judges had narrowed the field to two paintings. One depicted a beautiful bowl of fruit so vivid in appearance that birds flew down and tried to pluck grapes from the canvas. By contrast, the other painting was drab and lifeless and portrayed nothing more than a closed curtain. When asked what was behind it, the artist said that he did not know. After lengthy deliberation, the judges, perhaps given more to philosophy than to art, awarded first place to the painting of the expressionless curtain. For, as they explained, though the fruit deceived the birds of the air, the closed veil mystified the wisest men of the city.

In a similar way, the mind of John was filled with wonder, as his vision of heaven continued, and he saw a closed book in the right hand of the One seated on the throne (5:1). Written within and on the back, indicative of its fullness, and sealed with seven seals to insure secrecy, much like a Roman will, the book contained a complete account of the final destiny of the universe, as determined by God (cf., Psa. 139:16; Ezk.

45

2:10; Isa. 29:11; Dan. 8:26; Dan. 12:4). But when the apostle hears a great angel call for someone to come and open the book (5:2; cf., 10:1; 18:21) and realizes that no one "in heaven, or on earth, or under the earth" is good enough to receive the message (5:3; cf., Ex. 20:4), he begins to weep (5:4). It appears that the counsels of God for the consummation of history will not be disclosed, or His will executed.

At this point, one of the elders comforted John by telling him not to cry, for "the Lion that is from the tribe of Judah, the Root of David, has overcome so as to open the book and its seven seals" (5:5). This mighty Messiah is the One foreseen by Jacob when, in blessing his sons, he called Judah "a lion's whelp" through whom "the scepter shall not depart . . . until Shiloh comes" (Gen. 49:8–10).[1] He is the One described by Isaiah as the "root of Jesse, Who will stand as a signal for the peoples" (Isa. 11:10)—"in Him shall the Gentiles hope" (Rom. 15:12), "and His resting place will be glorious" (Isa. 11:10; cf., Isa. 11:1).

As John looks to the throne, he sees, amid the living creatures and the elders, not one with the qualities of a lion, but One like unto a lamb who had been slain (Isa. 53:7), the marks of sacrifice clearly visible (cf., John 20:20,25,27).[2] Yet the

---

[1] That Judah would be selected to bear the seed of the promised Messiah is quite significant. He is not one of the natural children of Rachel, like Joseph or Benjamin, whom we might have expected to receive the inheritance. And like his brethren, he was at one time a man given to the lower instincts of the flesh (e.g., Gen. 38:1–38). But there must have been something more commendable in his life, for later he is the son of Jacob who offers to give himself as a security for the life of Joseph (Gen. 43:3–10; Gen. 44:14–34). What stands out most to me, however, is the name. *Judah* means "praise of the Lord," and he was so named at birth by his mother, Leah (Gen. 29:35; Gen. 49:8). In a spiritual sense, this should characterize all the children of God. Such Jews are indeed a tribe, of which Jesus is the Head.

[2] Jesus is called a Lamb by John twenty-nine times in Revelation, a figure reminiscent of his account of the Baptist crying, "Behold, the Lamb of God who takes away the sin of the world!" (John 1:29).

Lamb is standing; the One slain is alive and standing on His feet, indicative of His resurrection life and readiness to act. He has "seven horns," symbolic of perfect strength (5:6; cf., Zech. 4:10). The Crucifixion has turned into glory.

When this mighty One came forward and took the book "out of the right hand of Him who sat on the throne" (5:7),[3] the four living creatures and the twenty-four elders fell down before the Lamb. The elders have harps—traditional instruments used to praise God (Psa. 33:2; Psa. 43:4; 1 Chron. 25:6; Isa. 24:8)—and they also carry golden bowls full of incense, symbolizing the gathered prayers of the saints (5:8; cf., 8:4; Psa. 141:2; Deut. 33:10; 2 Chron. 4:22). Prayer on earth ascends to the throne of God like the sweet savor of burnt offering, saturating heaven with the fragrance of devotion.

## A New Song

In this atmosphere of holy communion, the celestial creatures join in singing, "Worthy art Thou to take the book, and to break its seals; for Thou wast slain, and didst purchase for God with Thy blood men from every tribe and tongue and people and nation" (5:9).[4] It is called "a new song" because that which Christ has accomplished is wholly different and superior to the old covenant; nothing like it has ever existed before.[5] New works of grace call forth new songs of praise

---

[3] The word here for *came* is in the aorist tense, indicating completed action—He came forth, decisively and finally, in His death and Resurrection; whereas the word *took* is in the perfect tense, indicating that the completed act has a continuing effect; that is, having taken the book, He still holds it—history is still in Christ's hands.

[4] It might be observed that the elders are not singing of their own purchase, as indicated in the King James Version: "thou ... hast redeemed *us* to God. ...." The better rendering of this passage uses the words *men, them,* and *they* instead of "us" and "we."

[5] The word for *new* does not mean something new in time or origin, as if to imply previous nonexistence. There is a word to express that idea.

(Psa. 33:3; Psa. 40:3; Psa. 96:1; Psa. 98:1; Isa. 42:10, al.). The Christian life is always new, filled with new joy, new peace, new love, new vistas of the new Jerusalem.

Christ's worthiness in carrying out the divine purposes rests upon His sacrificial death, by which mankind was purchased for God. Without the offering up of His own life on Calvary, there could have been no redemption of the world, and Christ would have entered heaven alone. The cross thus becomes the basis for adoration.

This theme is amplified in the reference to the blood, and it lies at the heart of true worship.[6] For thousands of years, the slain Lamb had been foreshadowed in the ceremonial sacrifices of devout Jews, by which an innocent and unblemished victim was offered to God in the place of another. When the sacrificer fully identified with the shed blood, as if it were in fact his own, the offering expressed, more eloquently than

---

The term here speaks of a newness in nature, "new in the qualitative sense of something previously unknown, unprecedented, marvelous." For example, the word is used to give expression to the "new testament" of Christ's blood (Matt. 26:28; Mark 14:24; Luke 22:20; 1 Cor. 11:25), or the "new creature" Christ makes in redemption (2 Cor. 5:17; Gal. 6:15). It is also the word employed to describe "the new heaven and the new earth" (21:1; cf. 2 Peter 3:13), the "new Jerusalem" (21:2), and the new works of God (21:5). Colin Brown, ed., *The New International Dictionary of New Testament Theology* II (Grand Rapids: Zondervan, 1977), pp. 669, 670; cf. Gerhard Kittel and Gerhard Friedrich, eds., *Theological Dictionary of the New Testament* III (Grand Rapids: Wm. B. Eerdmans, 1966), p. 447.

[6] Blood is specifically mentioned 460 times in the Scripture. If related concepts were considered—such as atonement, priesthood, altar, covenant, sacrifice, and many others, all of which imply the shedding of blood—I doubt if there is a page in the Bible which does not have some reference to this source of life given unto death. It is the scarlet thread that weaves the whole scope of God's written Word into one harmonious witness to the Gospel of redeeming grace. For a comprehensive study of this concept, *see* Robert E. Coleman, *Written in Blood* (Old Tappan: Fleming H. Revell Co., 1972).

words, a heart in full conformity to the will of God. Equally precious, the blood on the altar displayed God's reception of the sacrifice and was therefore a witness of His grace, whereby He disclosed His merciful purpose to save a people. Though His holy nature demanded death for sin, the blood said that God so loved the world that He was willing to bear the judgment of His own law, by taking its consequences upon Himself.

The Old Testament sacrifices, of course, were but a promise of that perfect One to come. They all spoke of the day when God Himself would offer His own blood at the cross. Recall that it was during the Passover feast, while the paschal lambs were being slain in the temple, that Jesus was led outside the city and crucified. There for three hours He hung, the blood draining from His pierced hands and feet. As His breathing came harder and His body convulsed in pain, at last He lifted his voice and cried, "It is finished," signifying that everything typified in the ceremonial observances was completed. The work was done. Once and for all, Jesus, in our stead, offered His blood to God, "as of a lamb unblemished and spotless" (1 Peter 1:19).

Through His death, our redemption was effected (Matt. 20:28; Eph. 1:7). The word *redemption* means to buy back that which was in bondage. It was commonly used to designate the price of a slave, or in a slightly different way, it might refer to a ransom supplied for the release of a captive (Mark 10:45; 1 Tim. 2:6). In this context, the purchase price for the human race is Christ's blood, which cancels the liability of iniquity. By satisfying this just claim, inherent in the nature of God, Christ broke hell's shackles and His creature—man—was loosed from the law of sin and death.

The value of that which is purchased is not in itself, but in the price of its redemption. Think of what this means to the blood-bought ones! Their value can only be measured by the worth of the Son of God. How appropriate that this worth is not forgotten in heaven.

The ransomed ones come from "every tribe and tongue and people and nation." In contrast to the exclusive character of Judaism, as well as many other ethnic and religious bodies, the family of God transcends all cultural, linguistic, racial, and national boundaries. The worldwide nature of the gathering indicates, too, that Christ's great commission is fulfilled. The Gospel has reached all strata of society, unto the uttermost parts of the earth (cf., Matt. 24:14; Matt. 28:19; Mark 16:15; Acts 1:8).

As a result of their redemption, the heavenly beings sing, "Thou hast made them to be a kingdom and priests to our God; and they will reign upon the earth" (5:10). Thus is fulfilled the word spoken through Moses at Sinai, "You shall be to Me a kingdom of priests and a holy nation" (Ex. 19:6). What an exalted position! As a kingdom, Christ's purchased possession participates in His rule; and as priests, His people wait upon Him in perpetual service (cf., 20:4; 1 Thess. 4:15; 1 Cor. 15:51,52; Zech. 6:13).[7] Whether the reign be understood as present or future, followers of the Lamb live in the dignity of kingship and the purity of the priesthood.

**Life in Christ**

All this, and more, is ours through the cross of Christ. Indeed, He has given us His very life. "He who eats My flesh and drinks My blood," He said, "abides in Me, and I in him" (John 6:56). There is an actual partaking of His nature, so that we live and move and have our being in Him.

This life is transmitted by the Spirit, who accomplishes in us what Christ has done for us. "It is the Spirit who gives life; the flesh profits nothing" (John 6:63). Just as He presented the

---

[7] No useful purpose is served in trying to make a distinction between the kingdom and the church, though there are academic differences. Suffice to observe that, in a general sense, the kingdom relates to God's reign over His people, whereas the church is the fellowship of the redeemed living under Christ's authority.

blood of the Lamb without spot to God, so now the eternal
Spirit makes efficacious the merit of that sacrifice (Heb. 9:14;
cf., Heb. 10:29; Eph. 2:13).

Our part is to believe, to appropriate the life-renewing
power of the cross. At its heart is personal trust and reliance
in God, not as mere credence, but as a total commitment of
being. The believing person does not hold back, but completely gives himself to the object of his faith, so vividly sym-
bolized in the pouring out of life in blood sacrifice. One so
emptied of self becomes identified with the altar, a symbol of
God's dwelling place, and partakes of its nature. The word
*believe* actually goes back to a root in the Sanskrit, meaning
"to unite life," as in fusing one life with another.[8] It involves
taking new virtue into the soul, as eating and drinking bring
sustenance to the body. To believe thus, opens the way for
the Spirit to recreate life according to the divine purpose.

The accent throughout is upon God's enabling grace:
nothing deserved, nothing earned; redemption is solely the
unmerited gift of eternal love. Jesus literally paid it all. All
man can do is quit the futile game of pretending to be self-
sufficient, affirm the completed work of Christ, and by simple
faith receive the transfusion of the Saviour's life.

In one of Tennyson's letters, written from the village of
Noblethorpe, in Lincolnshire, he told of staying in the home
of two devout Methodists. Upon arriving at the house, he
asked his hostess for news. "Why, Mr. Tennyson," she replied, "there's only one piece of news that I know: that
Christ died for all men."

Somewhat surprised, the renowned poet responded,
"Well, that's old news and good news and new news."

Indeed, this is news that never gets old, not even in eter-

---

[8] George Curtis develops this thought in his monumental work, *Principles of Greek Etymology* (London: J. Murray, 1886), brought to my attention by Frank Robbins, *Revelation: Three Viewpoints* (Nashville:
Broadman, 1977), pp. 169, 170. Other helpful background reading on the
meaning of faith will be found in Colin Brown, op. cit., I, pp. 588–606.

nity. It is the remembrance of this matchless Gospel that
makes the celestial hosts burst into a new song, and the sound
is sweeter each time it is heard. To think that God—the infinite Lord of glory—so loved His rebellious race that He gave
His only begotten Son, to bear our sins in His body on the
tree, that whoever believes in Him shall not perish, but have
everlasting life. Amazing! This wondrous miracle of grace!
God has wrought redemption for the world, and those who
behold the Lamb never get over it.

Praise Him! praise Him! Jesus, our blessed Redeemer!
    Sing, O earth, His wonderful love proclaim!
Hail Him! hail Him! highest archangels in glory,
    Strength and honor give to His holy name!
Like a shepherd Jesus will guard His children,
    In His arms He carries them all day long:
Praise Him! praise Him! tell of His excellent greatness!
    Praise Him! praise Him! ever in joyful song!

Praise Him! praise Him! Jesus, our blessed Redeemer!
    For our sins He suffered and bled and died;
He our Rock, our hope of eternal salvation,
    Hail Him! hail Him! Jesus the Crucified.
Sound His praises, Jesus who bore our sorrows,
    Love unbounded, wonderful, deep and strong:
Praise Him! praise Him! tell of His excellent greatness!
    Praise Him! praise Him! ever in joyful song!

FANNY J. CROSBY

# 4

# *The Angels' Chorale*

"Worthy is the Lamb that was slain to receive power and riches and wisdom and might and honor and glory and blessing."

REVELATION 5:12

## Myriads of Angels

In some of the medieval monasteries following the custom in the temple of Israel, it was a rule that hymns of praise to God would never cease. When one of the monks would stop singing, another would pick up the song. Thus, day and night, the joyous sound was heard.

On one occasion a monastery was overrun by a band of Norse raiders. They slaughtered the monks without mercy, including the one who was singing. However, one monk was able to escape and hide in an inaccessible spot, where the attackers were not likely to find him. But when he heard the song of praise cease, instinctively he took it up, thus betraying his place of refuge.

Such an attitude toward continuous adoration may strike us as being rather rigid. But before we become critical, we should ponder the unceasing praise in heaven. For as soon as the chorus of the living creatures and elders concludes, John "looked" and "heard" another mighty voice around the throne (5:11). The perception of the eye, as well as the ear, a customary practice of the seer, intensifies the recognition (e.g., 22:8).

It is the angels who now join the heavenly song.[1] These spiritual beings appear repeatedly throughout the Bible as servants of God. They encamp around those who fear Him (Psa. 34:7), keeping them safe in God's appointed journeys (e.g., Gen. 24:40; Ex. 23:20; Psa. 91:11). Often they are the agents of divine deliverance in times of trouble (e.g., Dan. 6:22; Num. 20:16; Isa. 63:9). As "ministering spirits, sent out to render service for the sake of those who will inherit salvation" (Heb. 1:14), angels especially have an interest in the evangelization of the world (1 Peter 1:12; 1 Cor. 4:9). This role might explain why they figure so prominently in the witness of the early church in the Acts of the Apostles (e.g., Acts 5:19; Acts 8:26; Acts 10:3; Acts 12:7,8,15,23; Acts 27:23).

Their presence receives particular notice in connection with Christ's own ministry. Angels announce His birth (Luke 1:26,27; Luke 2:8–15; Matt. 1:20,21); they direct His flight to Egypt (Matt. 2:13,19,20); they minister to Him in the wilderness (Matt. 4:11); they strengthen Him during His travail of prayer in Gethsemane (Luke 22:43); they roll away the stone of His grave (Matt. 28:2) and tell the good news of His resurrection (Matt. 28:5–7; John 20:12,13); they assure the disciples of His ascension to the throne (Acts 1:10,11). Entering heaven, He was seen of angels (1 Tim. 3:16); and in the day of His glorious return, He will be accompanied by innumerable legions of angels (Matt. 16:27; Matt. 25:27; Mark 8:38; Luke 9:26; 2 Thess. 1:7).

Thus it is not surprising to note the frequent reference to

---

[1] It has been argued that angels cannot join the new song, for as unfallen creatures, they have not been born again. In fact, the point may be made that angels are not said to sing at all, but rather to speak their praise. Be that as it may, it is clear that angels celebrate the redemption of others. As to the way they express themselves, some translations of this passage render their utterance as song, including the New International Version, the Living Bible, and Today's English Version.

angels in the Revelation of Christ. One dispatched the message to John (1:2; 22:16). Each of the seven churches has an angel (1:20; 2:1,8,12,18; 3:1,7,14). It was an angel who inquired if someone was worthy to open and read the book (5:2). Angels are the proclaimers and executors of God's judgments (8:6,7; 9:11,15,16; 10:1,26; 12:7; 14:6,8,9,10,15,18, 19; 15:1; 17:1,5; 18:2,21; 19:17; 20:12). On the other hand, angels are there to seal the elect (7:1–4) and assist in their prayers (8:3–5), just as they unveil the new Jerusalem (21:9) and guard the gates of the city (21:19). Yet, for all their importance, they are careful to point out their creatureliness and to forbid worship of themselves (22:8,9)

In the present scene, the angels surround the throne, perhaps forming an outer circle around the living creatures and elders. Their number is "myriads of myriads, and thousands of thousands," a way of saying that the number is incalculable (5:11). It is similar to Daniel's description of the vast host in heaven, ministering to the Ancient of Days (Dan. 7:10). That the myriads of angels are represented as a single voice indicates a harmony of emotion and feeling, as they lift their song in antiphonal praise.

## Worthy Is the Lamb

"Worthy is the Lamb that was slain," they cry (5:12). As had the representatives of creation and redemption before them, the faithful servants of heaven declare the worthiness of Him who was nailed to the cross. In keeping with their position, they do not address the Lamb directly, but adopt a more distant form of expression, using the third person.

Remember that the holy angels never lost their created glory through sin and hence do not need redemption. However, as the created ministers of God, they have watched, with excited anticipation, the divinely initiated program unfold from the beginning. Though the atoning death of Christ

did not alter directly their own unfallen nature, still the
angels shared its joy, knowing that by Christ's sacrifice,
countless sons of men were liberated from the chains of
death, made into a holy and royal priesthood, and destined to
a position of privilege higher than their own.[2] There is no
jealousy in heaven. What brings fulfillment to one is shared
by all, for it is God's doing, and His glory is their greatest
pleasure. Charles Wesley caught something of this wonder
when he wrote:

> Angels rejoice in Jesus' grace
> And vie with man's more favored race:
> The blood that did for us atone
> Conferred on you some gift unknown;
> Your joy through Jesus' pains abounds,
> Ye triumph by His glorious wounds.
>
> Him ye beheld, our conqu'ring God,
> Returned with garments rolled in blood!
> Ye saw, and kindled at the sight,
> And filled with shouts the realms of light;
> With loudest hallelujahs met,
> And fell, and kissed the bleeding feet.

Reflecting this perfection of His work, the angels offer the
Lamb a sevenfold tribute of "power and riches and wisdom
and might and honor and glory and blessing" (5:12). In the
original text, all the words are introduced by a single article,
indicating that they stand together as one. The first four

---

[2] Men, unlike angels, were created to be sons of God, not mere servants, and hence can know a superior intimacy of relationship. In some
bodily characteristics, such as strength, humans are "a little lower" than
angels (Heb. 2:7,9), but even this shall be changed when the body is
glorified in the final resurrection (Luke 20:36). For a very readable discussion of this whole subject, *see* Billy Graham's *Angels: God's Secret
Agents* (New York: Doubleday Co., Inc., 1975), pp. 35–47.

speak of attributes that belong to Christ, while the last three relate more to an attitude toward Him.

*Power* speaks of the Lamb's unlimited ability to perform. He is the availing might of God (Eph. 1:19; 1 Cor 1:24). Nothing can withstand the force of His sovereign will.

To Him also belongs wealth. The word *riches* denotes infinite resources and fullness of every divine gift. All the treasures of the universe are His. O "the unfathomable riches of Christ!" (Eph. 3:8; cf., Eph. 1:7; Eph. 3:16; Rom. 2:4; Rom. 9:23; Rom. 11:33).

Next comes *wisdom*, that mental excellence to know the highest ends and the best means to their attainment. That Christ would give Himself to die for sinners, an act considered utterly foolish by the world's estimate of brilliance, is the supreme disclosure of wisdom from above (1 Cor. 1:18; 1 Cor. 2:8,14; 1 Cor. 3:18–23).

*Strength*, too, is His possession. Stronger than the forces of evil, He can disarm any foe and conquer any enemy (Luke 11:22; Eph. 6:10). There is no circumstance over which He is not master.

Appropriately responding to His greatness, the Lamb is worthy of *honor*, the highest esteem of public distinction that can be conferred; it is an eminence that excels all others (Heb. 2:9; Acts 2:33; 1 Peter 1:21).

Akin to this truth, but emphasizing more the element of divine splendor, is the *glory* that the Lamb receives. It is that luminous manifestation attending the presence of God, so that to behold Him is to see the very Shechinah of the majesty on high (John 1:14; John 2:11; John 17:22,24; 2 Peter 1:16–18).

Climaxing the pryamiding of words is the word *blessing*— that praise which belongs to the Son by virtue of who He is and what He has done (Mark 11:9,10; Rom. 15:29). Inherent in it is the awareness that everything—of which mankind's redemption is the most personal—is rightfully His, and thus it calls forth grateful acknowledgment by all His subjects.

William Barclay observes that "it is the one gift that we who have nothing can give to Him who possesses all."[3]

The song has many ingredients of David's praise before his people, as their offerings for the temple were presented to God:

> ... Blessed art Thou, O Lord God of Israel our father, forever and ever. Thine, O Lord, is the greatness and the power and the glory and the victory and the majesty, indeed everything that is in the heavens and the earth; Thine is the dominion, O Lord, and Thou dost exalt Thyself as head over all. Both riches and honor come from Thee, and Thou dost rule over all, and in Thy hand is power and might; and it lies in Thy hand to make great, and to strengthen everyone. Now therefore, our God, we thank Thee, and praise Thy glorious name.
>
> 1 Chronicles 29:10–13

Having extolled the greatness of his Lord, the king proceeded to affirm the moral uprightness in which God delighted, concluding with the prayer that his people, and especially his son, might always "direct their heart to Thee." When he finished, the whole assembly was called upon to follow his example and "bless the Lord" (1 Chron. 29:14–20).

## The Wonder of Worship

It is beautiful to contemplate the nature of deity and to bask in His glory. This is really what worship is—the adoring response of the creature to the infinite majesty of God. While it presupposes submission to Him, worship, in its highest sense, is not supplication for needs, or even thanksgiving for blessings, but "the occupation of the soul with God Himself."[4] Whatever the means—preaching and hearing of the

---

[3] William Barclay, *The Revelation of John* I, rev. ed. (Philadelphia: Westminster Press, 1976), p. 180.

[4] Huber L. Drumwright, Jr., and R. Allan Killen, "Worship," *Wycliffe Bible Encyclopedia* II (Chicago: Moody Press, 1975), p. 1823.

Word, celebration of the sacraments, singing ~~~~~~~~~
ing of prayers, quiet meditation—the end of it ~~~~~~~~
joy of magnifying the One who alone is worthy.

Such devotion should become a perpetual atti~~~~
heart, permeating every thought, so that all of h~~~~
with a sense of the numinous. The hymnist voiced ~~~~ ~~ll,
when he wrote:

> Lord, arm me with Thy Spirit's might,
>> Since I am called by Thy great name,
> In Thee my wand'ring thoughts unite,
>> Of all my works be Thou the aim:
> Thy love attend me all my days,
> And my sole business be Thy praise.[5]

In experiencing true worship, however, we can never lose
sight of the Lamb who was slain. The manifestation of God in
this expression of His grace is the supreme revelation of the
redeeming Word, whereby—through the Spirit—we are
brought near to the throne. To see Him on the cross is to
know that God loves us and has borne our sins away.

The story is told of a traveler who looked for unusual
things in the cities he visited. During a tour of a town one
day, he was attracted by a remarkable spire over a public
building. Turning to see it better, he noticed, about two-
thirds of the way up, a stone figure of a lamb on the wall.

The man stopped a passerby, to ask if there was some significance to the lamb's stone replica. Told that it marked the
place from which a workman lost his balance and fell while
the building was under construction, the traveler inquired,
"Was he killed?"

"No," said the local resident, "it was a miracle. When his
friends hurried down, expecting to find the mangled body on

---

[5] From John Wesley's hymn, "O God, What Offering Shall I Give."

...he pavement, there he was, shaken and badly bruised, but with hardly a bone broken. It happened that several lambs were on their way to slaughter, and as the mason fell, he landed on the back of one of them. The lamb was killed, of course, but his soft body broke the mason's fall and saved his life. The builder was so impressed with the miracle that he had that stone lamb placed there, as a lasting tribute."[6]

We can surmise the traveler's reaction to such a story. But what must have been in the mind of the mason whose life was spared?

Perhaps somewhat akin to his feeling was the wonder of the angels, when they beheld the Lamb ascending to the throne of heaven. As Wesley envisioned:

> Ye saw Him in the courts above
> With all His recent prints of love—
> The wounds!—The blood! Ye heard its voice
> That heightened all your highest joys;
> Ye felt it sprinkled through the skies,
> And shared that better sacrifice.

How much more must be the feelings of gratitude in the hearts of those who actually are redeemed by the Lamb's sacrifice, not as an accident of fate, but by the deliberate offering of Himself for the world. Well did the singer conclude:

> Not angel tongues can e'er express
> Th' unutterable happiness;
> Nor human hearts can e'er conceive
> The blessing wherein through Christ ye live;
> But all your heaven, ye glorious powers,
> And all your God, is doubly ours!

CHARLES WESLEY

---

[6] A favorite illustration of Dr. Herbert Lockyer, Sr., appearing in *Moody Monthly*, November 1954, p. 40.

# 5

# *The Crescendo of the Universe*

"To Him who sits on the throne, and to the Lamb, be blessing and honor and glory and dominion forever and ever ... Amen."

REVELATION 5:13,14

## Every Living Thing

"When I think of God," wrote composer Franz Joseph Haydn, "my heart is so full of joy that the notes leap and dance as they leave my pen."[1] Such must have been the experience of John, as he continued to behold the celebration around the throne of heaven. The joy seems to bound from the script like a rollicking child at play, gathering force and momentum, until finally it is caught up by "every created thing which is in heaven and on the earth and on the sea, and all things in them" (5:13). It is an exclamation now embracing the whole universe, in which no creature is excluded.

The totality of the description suggests that there are other rational beings in heaven besides the angels, elders, and seraphim, and though their nature and function may be different, they, too, want to join the heavenly song. Some scholars have conjectured that the praise might also include the physical bodies of creation, such as the sun, moon, and stars. We do know that the whole creation groans, waiting for the day when it will be set free from its bondage of decay, and have its share in that magnificent liberty that can only belong to the children of God (*see* Rom. 8:22,23).

---

[1] Franz Joseph Haydn, cited in *Decision*, July 1961, p. 15.

The host not only encompasses all embodied creatures of heaven, earth, and sea, but also embraces those in the subterranean parts of the earth (5:13). Is this only a poetic expression, using a fourfold reiteration to emphasize the universality of the creaturely praise? Or is it to be taken as descriptive of the spirits of those who have died outside of the covenant of grace?[2] Support can be found for either point of view.

If we hold to the latter, an interesting question is raised, regarding those members of the race who have received no Gospel presentation, or having heard, have rejected its demands. Can there be a recognition of Christ through natural revelation, limited though it may be; or is there implied a universal perception of His glory in the afterlife, either through honest reflection upon previous knowledge or through additional illumination? Can those creatures who have died in unbelief rise up to praise Him?

This would seem to be the more literal explanation of this phrase. So great is the accomplishment of God's redeeming Word, so shattering His conquest of evil through the cross, that even those who pierced Him, who conspired to kill Him, by divine constraint will lift their voices to acknowledge that the One they scorned on earth is none other than the Prince of heaven, the Messiah of God. One can only imagine how those rebels must feel who concur in this universal acclaim with bitter pangs of remorse, knowing that they no longer have recourse to divine mercy. There are profound theologi-

---

[2] It was commonly accepted by the Jews that the souls of the dead entered Sheol, a place under the earth sometimes called "the pit" (Isa. 38:18; cf., Psa. 6:5; Psa. 28:1; Psa. 30:9). Prior to the victorious death of Christ, this place of the departed included those who died in faith and were in paradise (Luke 16:22; Luke 23:43; cf., Num. 27:13). However, Christ led those who were waiting in this captivity into His own abode, now to be with Him. So the allusion here to "under the earth" could have reference to those still in the realm of the dead and hence outside the kingdom of righteousness.

cal questions here, to be sure. But it is nonetheless affirmed that someday "every knee" shall bow before Him, every creature "in heaven, and on earth, and under the earth," and "every tongue" shall confess "that Jesus Christ is Lord, to the glory of God the Father" (Phil. 2:10,11).

## Eternal Blessing

The song rises "to Him that sits on the throne, and to the Lamb" (5:13), joining the two in equal worship, while emphasizing their reign over all things. The One seated in ruling majesty upon His throne and the slain Lamb, who bore our sins away, hold the key to history and the future. In their sovereign will, all creation is guided to its destination of holy worship.

The close relationship between God and the Lamb comes out again and again in Revelation. They are cojoined in administering judgment upon the world (6:16). To them are attributed the firstfruits of redemption (14:1,4). Together they constitute the illumination of heaven (21:22,23), while out of them proceeds the pure river of the water of life (22:1,3). And, as in this song, both appear in another throne celebration, with its accompanying blessing (7:9,10,17).

The importance of keeping the second person of the Godhead in focus cannot be missed. As "the image of the invisible God, the firstborn of all creation," He has fulfilled the purpose for which all things came into being and to which all things are moving (Col. 1:15–17; cf., Rom. 11:36). Yet His identity as the Lamb continually keeps before us the centrality of His work of redemption. We can never come to God except through the shed blood of His Son.[3] He who would know the Father must first bow at the foot of the cross.

---

[3] The representation of Christ at the throne as the Lamb, while a clear picture of His redemptive mission, avoids a direct anthropomorphism or man-centered analogy and requires imagination for the figure to be transposed to the human situation. Perhaps this is purposely designed,

To this holy union "be blessing and honor and glory and dominion forever and ever" (5:13). The little word *be* underscores the continuous and ever-present nature of the qualities that follow; they are inseparable from His Being. The fourfold affirmation, as observed in the use of the number elsewhere, stresses the universality of the adoration. Of the attributes chosen, all correspond to those mentioned in the previous song of the angels (5:12), except that a different word, denoting superior might or dominion, is used here for *power*. Also, all four are preceded by a definite article, making it literally, "the blessing and the glory and the honor and the dominion," which gives a separate emphasis to each quality; in contrast, the seven attributes of the former group are introduced with a single article, making the whole list read as one word.

The familiar designation of eternity concludes the song, "forever and ever." It could be rendered "to the ages of ages," or "timeless ages." The praise of God never ends. It is the ceaseless response of every form of life "to Him who sits on the throne, and to the Lamb."

Culminating the scene of worship, the living creatures, unable to find words to express any higher adoration, simply keep saying, "Amen" (5:14). Their response might be translated in such a way as to imply that it is voiced after each of the seven attributes spoken by the angels, and also after the four shouted by creation. In any event, it is apparent that this sequence of tributes ends with those who began it (4:8). As the cherubim continue chanting their accent, the four and twenty elders fall down and worship Him "that lives forever" (5:14).[4]

---

consistent with the tenor of Revelation, to enhance the "otherness" of God's Being and thereby increase the sense of wonder and awe.

[4] The phrase "that lives forever and ever," found in some manuscripts, is omitted in most newer versions.

## All People Must Come

The universal dimension of this scene is breathtaking. How God will bring forth His praise from every creature in the next life is not explained, but it surely puts a high premium upon the Gospel mandate in this present world. As to those who have died without hearing the saving Word, that is a matter beyond our jurisdiction. It is enough to know that they are in the hands of a just and merciful God. The challenge before us is the multiplied millions in our own generation who do not know the Lamb. Just as someday we must all affirm His glory, so no one can escape the reach of Calvary.

The cross demands a response, first in submission to its claims, then in witness to its power. Everyone for whom the Saviour died must be told. The blood that brought us to God cries out for everyone to come.

The careless way that many of us regard this responsibility may raise the question of how sincerely we take the message to heart. When Charles Peace, the infamous criminal, was offered by the prison chaplain "the consolations of religion" on his way to the scaffold, the wretched man turned upon him and exclaimed, "Do you believe it? Do you believe it?" Then, with obvious bitterness, he cried: "If I believed that, I would crawl across England on broken glass on my hands and knees to tell men it was true."[5]

Indeed, if we really believe that Christ is God and that He died to save the world, then we cannot sit idly by while multitudes perish. Jesus is the only way whereby we can come to the Father. This message must be heard, else there is no hope for mankind.

To some persons this assertion seems arrogant. What right have we to impose our beliefs upon others, they ask. A man once said to Dr. R. A. Torrey, "I'm not a Christian, but I am

---

[5] Quoted by G. Ray Jordan, *The Supreme Possession* (New York: Abingdon-Cokesbury, 1945), p. 45.

moral and upright. I would like to know what you have
against me." Torrey looked the man in the eye and replied, "I
charge you, sir, with treason against heaven's King!"[6]

That is the issue which must be faced. It is not finally our
Gospel, but His. And because Jesus Christ is Lord, before
Him every knee will bow. It is in that obeisance that we go
forth to herald the King's message.

Ultimately, however, it is not a sense of obedience to His
command, or the call of human need, that constrains the witness. Such motivation alone becomes brittle and in time
grows weary in well-doing. Supremely, it is the love of Christ
Himself, the consuming desire that God be glorified, that
impels one to tell the old, old story of redeeming grace.

I know a man who for many years has gone out on the
streets and preached the Gospel, though often only a few
people gather to listen; not infrequently, he is made an object
of scorn. Asked why he keeps going, in view of such little appreciation, he answered, "Oh, you do not understand. I'm not
out here to please the people. I'm here to praise the Lord
with the angels."

That's the spirit that puts a shout into any activity,
whether it is preaching on the street corner, writing a paper
at the office, washing dishes at home, fixing a flat tire on the
highway, or singing in the choir at church. With such an attitude, one can never despair or take offense when slighted.
For whatever is done, great or small, it is rendered as unto
the Lord; the deed becomes an act of worship.

Such devotion is not dependent upon moods, impressions,
forms, ceremonies, being with the right homogeneous group,
or any other extraneous support. These things may contribute
to the atmosphere, but worship itself is not engineered by
human devices; it is kindled in the trusting heart of the con-
trite believer by the Spirit of God.

---

[6] Portrait of R. A. Torrey in *Great Gospel Sermons* I (New York:
Fleming H. Revell Co., 1949), p. 138.

A remarkable outpouring of the Spirit occurred at Asbury College a few years ago, in which the Presence of the Lord was so manifest that classes had to be dismissed, extracurricular activity came to a standstill, and for eight days and nights, almost everyone joined in spontaneous worship. There were no advertisements, no distinguished speakers, no organized program—just the commanding sense of the divine Spirit. Something of the feeling was illustrated in the reaction of three ladies from a distant city, who visited the campus during this period. A few minutes after they walked into the college auditorium, one of them said, "I must take off my shoes, for this is holy ground." She suited her actions to her words and, along with her two companions, walked forward in stocking feet to kneel at the altar.[7]

In a symbolical way, that is how everyone feels in the Presence of the King. One wants only to bow before Him and, with all the universe, join in the praise of the Lamb. In this holy communion, our love unites with His, quickening a desire to mount the housetops and herald His name to the ends of the earth and to the farthest star.

> From all that dwell below the skies,
> Let the Creator's praise arise;
> Let the Redeemer's name be sung,
> Through every land by every tongue.
>
> Eternal are thy mercies, Lord;
> Eternal truth attends thy word:
> Thy praise shall sound from shore to shore,
> Till suns shall rise and set no more.
>
> Your lofty themes, ye mortals, bring;
> In songs of praise divinely sing;

---

[7] This and many other stories about this revival may be found in Robert E. Coleman, ed., *One Divine Moment* (Old Tappan: Fleming H. Revell Co., 1970).

The great salvation loud proclaim,
And shout for joy the Saviour's name.

In every land begin the song;
To every land the strains belong;
In cheerful sounds all voices raise,
And fill the world with loudest praise.

ISAAC WATTS

# 6

## *The Martyrs' Canticle*

"How long, O Lord, holy and true, wilt Thou refrain from judging and avenging our blood on those who dwell on the earth?"

REVELATION 6:10

### A Suffering Church

With the cosmic triumph of Christ resounding throughout eternity, the Revelation turns back in time, to the events which are to transpire before the consummation of the kingdom. The vision pictures seven judgments that fall upon the earth (6:1–8:1), reflecting the doom prophesied to Israel, that God would multiply calamities seven times as sin increases (Lev. 26:18,21,24,28). Yet as the series of disasters unfolds, with all the attendant suffering, authority still rests with God. This fact is represented by the Lamb breaking the seals of the book, thereby unleashing the coming destruction (6:1). Whatever takes place in this world falls within the perimeters of the divine will.

Opening of the first four seals brings forth four horsemen, riding four different-colored steeds. The imagery comes out of Zechariah, where four horses are dispatched across the earth to revenge Israel's oppressors (Zech. 6:1–8; cf., Zech. 1:7–17). In the vision of John, the horses and their riders personify the evil forces abroad in the world. The leading horse is white, mounted by one wearing a crown of victory and carrying a bow symbolic of military power (6:2; cf., Jer. 51:56; Ezek. 39:3; Psa. 46:19). It suggests one of great emi-

69

nence, a pretender of Christ, going forth to conquer.[1] The
second horse is red, suggestive of bloodshed, and the rider
wields a great sword, to effect his carnage (6:3,4). The third
horseman, riding a black horse, is carrying a balance in his
hand, which indicates a scarcity of food and hardship (6:5,6;
cf., Lev. 26:26; Ezk. 4:16). The last horse is ashen in color,
and its rider's name is death, with Hades following him, to
gather the slain (6:7,8). These horsemen form a unit of devas-
tation which is said to reach a quarter of mankind. The calamities, together with the even more awful upheavals
disclosed by the opening of the sixth and seventh seals, recall
the judgments prophesied by Ezekiel (Ezk. 14:12–21), as well
as the events described by Jesus as occurring prior to His Second Coming (Matt. 24:4–31).

Amid this intensifying destruction upon the earth, as the
fifth seal is opened, the scene shifts again to heaven, and we
see "underneath the altar the souls of those who had been
slain because of the word of God, and because of the testimony which they had maintained" (6:9). These are persons
who have been martyred in the course of the preceding trials,
indicative of the world's hostility against the church. Many
Christians have died for the truth received from the Lord (cf.,
12:17; 20:4), and it would appear that such martyrdom will
increasingly become more common (cf. Matt. 24:9; Mark
13:9,13; Luke 21:12,18; John 16:2).

The altar recalls the place in the tabernacle and temple

---

[1] Some scholars interpret this crowned rider on the white horse to be
Christ Himself, paralleling this passage with pictures of Christ in
19:11–21. Others see the figure as representing the conquest of the Gospel or the Word of God, but these interpretations seem incongruous with
the opening of the other three seals, which clearly have evil connota-
tions. The similarity between the first horseman here and Christ, described later, illustrates the character of an Antichrist, seeking to
accomplish his devious ends by taking the guise of the true One (cf., 1
John 2:18,22; 1 John 4:3; 2 John 7).

where offerings were made to God. This had its eternal counterpart in heaven, from whence the pattern came (Ex. 25:9,40; Num. 8:4; Heb. 8:5; Heb. 9:23).[2] As the focus of the reconciling sacrifice, it was here that God and man would meet together in the covenant of His grace.

To speak of souls beneath the altar picks up on the belief that life was embodied in the blood (Lev. 17:11–14), so that in the slaying of the martyrs, it was as though their life was poured out unto God. Their blood ran down into the hollows below the altar, where it cries out as a witness against their murderers (Gen. 4:10; Matt. 23:29–36), even as it declares their faithfulness unto death (cf. Phil. 2:17; 2 Tim. 4:6; Rom. 12:1).

The scene is pictorial, of course, but it does establish that before the resurrection of the body, the souls of the Christian dead are in some kind of spiritual communication with the throne. We are not allowed to know what form it is, though judging from the way the martyrs are wearing robes, it would appear to be a body of substance, appropriate for its purpose (6:11). In this self-conscious state, these immaculately clothed saints are keenly aware of what is happening in the world and

---

[2] The word *altar*, used over 400 times in the Bible, comes from a root meaning "to slaughter." As the place of blood sacrifice, of course, the altar antedates the construction of the tabernacle, the first reference coming after the flood, when Noah offered sacrifices to God (Gen. 8:20). Subsequently, altars were built by Abraham, Isaac, Jacob, Moses, and Joshua. With the erection of the tabernacle, a brazen altar was made for the outer court; and an altar of incense, sometimes called the golden altar, was placed before the veil in the sanctuary. The Ark of the Covenant, adorned with the Mercy Seat, also constituted an altar in the Holy of Holies. These altars were constructed on a more elaborate scale in the later temples. The scenes of the altar in Revelation relate especially to the altar of incense, typifying the offering of prayer (8:3,5; 9:13; cf., 11:1; 14:18; 16:7). It has led some interpreters to think that this is the only altar in heaven, since the offering for sins has been finished. However, there is no reason to press the point, for any altar, by its nature, embodies the principle of sacrifice and meeting with God.

have an obvious concern for the soon completion of God's work.

## The Inevitable Question

Observing the continuing struggle of the church and the seemingly unrestrained attacks of evil men upon the righteous, the martyrs call out, with a loud voice, "How long, O Lord, holy and true, wilt Thou refrain from judging and avenging our blood on those who dwell on the earth?" (6:10). It is another way of voicing the Psalmist's question, "Lord, How long shall the wicked exult?" (Psa. 94:3).[3] After all, is not God in control, and can He not at any time intervene, to stop the brutal slaughter of His people? Why, then, does He permit those whose names are written in heaven to be afflicted by vicious inhabitants of the earth, sensual men who derive their values from the flesh and who have no concern but their own immediate gratification? (cf., 3:10; 8:13; 9:10; 13:8,12,14; 17:2,8).

It is a good question—one that honest hearts have been asking through the centuries, especially in times of adversity. That the query is heard even in heaven certainly absolves it from any sinful propensity. This is a natural cry of human nature in prolonged waiting, which in this setting rises to the very throne of the Most High, intoned with praises of His sovereignty.

God is addressed as "Lord," a term emphasizing "absolute ownership and uncontrolled power."[4] This mighty God, om-

---

[3] This question occurs in various forms through the Old Testament, for example, Psa. 6:3; Psa. 13:1,2; Psa. 35:17; Psa. 59:5; Psa. 79:5–10; Psa. 80:4; Psa. 89:46; Psa. 90:13; Psa. 94:3; Isa. 6:11; Jer. 47:6; Zeck. 1:12; Hab. 1:2, al.

[4] Joseph Henry Thayer, *A Greek-English Lexicon of the New Testament* (New York: American Book Co., 1886), p. 130. It is not the usual word for *Lord* in the Bible, but one of a more restricted usage, especially as referring to a master of slaves (cf., Luke 2:29; Acts 4:24; 2 Peter 2:1;

nipotent in authority, is also acclaimed as "holy and true." The recognition is very important, when the question before us is being considered. For whatever God elects to do, whether by giving or withholding deliverance, His holiness precludes any defilement of love, and His truthfulness eliminates any possibility of error. There is no doubt expressed; in these minds, there is no uncertainty about the ultimate victory. Though the continuing conflict is not comprehended, still the saints affirm that the ways of God are perfect; He can never make a mistake.

This sense of God's moral integrity helps us understand the spirit of the martyrs' request that He take care of their enemies. Theirs is not an uncaring attitude of personal vindictiveness, but a sincere desire for divine justice. There is probably an allusion to the practice of a plaintiff pleading his own cause in a Hebrew law court. Any failure of the judge to exonerate the plaintiff amounted to a decision in favor of the defendant.[5] In the case of the martyrs, they had been condemned by human courts, and in the eyes of men, that decision stands against them until reversed by a higher court. So they are asking that the Judge of the universe publicly show the rightness of their blood-sealed witness by putting an end to the tyranny which has tried to silence the message of God. In so doing, God will vindicate His own Word.

What is lacking in this song is not the note of worship, but of patience. This is apparent in the response to their cry, when the martyrs are given white robes and told to "rest for a little while longer, until the number of their fellow servants and their brethren who were to be killed even as they had been, should be completed also" (6:11). It was a reminder that the redemptive mission of God is still going on, and that

---

Jude 4); cf. Colin Brown, ed., *The New International Dictionary of New Testament Theology* II (Grand Rapids: Zondervan, 1967), pp. 508–520.

[5] This point is developed at length by G. B. Caird, *The Revelation of St. John the Divine* (New York: Harper & Row, 1966), p. 85.

it will not end until the purpose for which the Lamb was slain is known to the ends of the earth. Until then, the Lord is long-suffering, "not wishing for any to perish but for all to come to repentance" (2 Peter 3:9). Making known the Gospel of grace will be costly in lives, of course. God has already taken that into account, and He knows the number that will be martyred in the course of fulfilling His redemptive plan. But when contemplating the ultimate blessedness of the completed church, one can bear with joy the travail involved in reaching His objective. With ultimate victory to look forward to, the martyrs are told to rest. They can leave the matter of justice in the hands of their sovereign Lord. However long the dark period might be, it will pass away in the dawning of a new day. Their white robes, emblems of purity and victory, are a token of that assurance.

## Waiting in Confidence

The cry of the martyrs who long for the consummation of history reflects similar feelings in the suffering church on earth. We want to get God's work over in a hurry. In our clouded apprehension of His ways, we find difficulty in perceiving the vast extent of His world mission and the painstaking process of making a people in His own character, to praise Him forever. And God will not compromise His goals.

By placing this song in the narrative of earth's sorrows, God makes us aware that He will not circumvent means in accomplishing His ends. What we consider detours, hardships, even the pangs of death, often are the very things that God uses to conform us more perfectly to His image. If the Captain of our salvation learned obedience through His sufferings, how can we expect to understand Calvary love on beds of ease? (cf. Heb. 2:10; Heb. 15:8; 2 Tim. 2:12; 2 Cor. 4:17,18; Rom. 5:3–5). Let us beware, then, that we do not resist that which is for our own good. While we yearn for the day when trials will be over, God is interested in the blessedness of these sufferings, for apart from them, we can experience neither the depths of His character nor the full sufficiency of His grace. In God's plan, condescending to the limitations of fallen humanity, there are no shortcuts to true happiness. The way to His goal is long and hard—it leads through the wilderness and many attacks of the enemy. Somewhere, there is a cross in it. Crucifixion may be a slow death, but it is certain.[6]

Come what may, we can rest assured that nothing can happen to us without first passing through God's will. Not that He causes difficulties, but that, in His infinite wisdom, He can use them for His glory and even bring the wrath of men to praise Him. Too easily we get upset over the perilous conditions of the world. The way we sometimes wring our hands in exasperation and complaint would make one wonder if we really do believe that God is sovereign. Surely we cannot sit idly by when the harvest is waiting, nor can we rejoice when there is unconfessed sin in our lives.[7] But we should not despair when sufferings remain and even increase, for the "Lord, holy and true," is working through all these circumstances "for good to those who love God, to those who are called according to His purpose" (Rom. 8:28).

During World War I, a party was given for a group of soldiers who were soon going to the front. Near the close of

---

[6] Suffering love in the creature, when voluntarily accepted in God's economy, works to "the decentralization of the self" and thereby brings one into harmony with the moral and social structure of the universe. That is why only persons who have suffered are truly benevolent. For a thought-provoking treatment of this idea, see Paul E. Billheimer, *Don't Waste Your Sorrows* (Fort Washington: Christian Literature Crusade, 1977).

[7] Let it be clear that joy in all things comes when the heart is right with God, and not before. To pretend joy when there is none is hypocrisy. There is reason to anticipate blessing and by faith to praise God for it in the midst of adversity. But merely to rejoice, with no inward realization of personal cleansing, contradicts the nature of sin and can lead to deadly deception.

the program, a young officer rose to express appreciation for the entertainment. His remarks were cheerful, full of charm and humor. Then, suddenly as an afterthought before sitting down, using a different tone of voice, he said: "We are soon crossing to France. . . . and very possibly, of course, to death. Will any one of our friends here tell us how to die?"[8]

There was a stunned silence. It seemed that no one knew what to say. Finally, one of the singers who had taken part in the program came forward and, turning to the soldier, began to sing the great aria from Mendelssohn's *Elijah:*

> O rest in the Lord, wait patiently for Him,
> And He shall give thee thy heart's desires;
> Commit thy way unto Him, and trust in Him;
> And fret not thyself because of evil-doers.
> O rest in the Lord, wait patiently for Him,
> And He shall give thee thy heart's desires.

This is the message that all of us need, in facing the threatening vicissitudes of life. We cannot know what awaits us on this earth, but we can trust Him who holds all these things in His hand, and that is enough. He is our security. He is our comfort. He is our joy. And in His everlasting arms there is peace, perfect peace.

> God moves in a mysterious way,
>     His wonders to perform;
> He plants his footsteps in the sea,
>     And rides upon the storm.
>
> Deep in unfathomable mines
>     Of never-failing skill

---

[8] Substance of a story told by Bishop Moule, as reported by G. Ray Jordan, *The Supreme Possession* (New York: Abingdon-Cokesbury, 1945), pp. 186, 187.

He treasures up his bright designs,
 And works his sovereign will.

Judge not the Lord by feeble sense,
 But trust him for his grace;
Behind a frowning providence
 He hides a smiling face.

Blind unbelief is sure to err,
 And scan his work in vain;
God is his own interpreter,
 And he will make it plain.

WILLIAM COWPER

# 7

# *The Song of Salvation*

"Salvation to our God who sits on the throne, and to the Lamb."

REVELATION 7:10

## The Vast Multitude

A little girl, soon to undergo minor surgery, was told by the understanding doctor, "This will hurt, but you may cry as much as you please."

The young patient looked up at him bravely and replied: "I would rather sing." And she did, much to the dismay of those present, until the ordeal was over.

In the larger dimension of suffering, that is the attitude cultivated in the Revelation of Christ, as the church moves through the mounting tribulations of the world. With the opening of the sixth seal, the very forces of nature are loosed upon mankind; there is a great earthquake, the sun becomes black as sackcloth; the moon turns blood red; the stars fall to the earth like figs shaken from a tree before a strong gale; the sky vanishes like a scroll that is rolled up; every mountain and island is removed from its place (6:12–14). So frightening is the apocalyptic cataclysm that the people of the earth, from the highest rulers to the lowest slaves, run to caves and mountains, trying to find somewhere to hide from "the presence of Him who sits on the throne, and from the wrath of the Lamb" (6:15,16). The day of His anger has come, "and who is able to stand?" (6:17; cf., Nahum 1:6; Mal. 3:2; 1 Peter 4:18).

Answering this question, before the final seal is removed from the book of destiny, there is an interlude in which the church is reassured. Those who place their trust in the living God can stand unmoved through all the coming judgments. In a vision, John sees the saints on earth protected by the sealing of God's signet, guaranteeing them divine ownership and entrance into the heavenly city (7:1–3).[1] They are represented by the mystical figure of 144,000 from all the tribes of Israel, a symbolic way of emphasizing the comprehensive number secured through the terrible events of the end time (7:4–8). The depiction of the church as the new Israel finds support in Jesus' promise that His followers would one day "sit upon twelve thrones, judging the twelve tribes of Israel" (Matt. 19:28; cf., Luke 22:30). Likewise, Paul speaks of the church as the "Israel of God" (Gal. 6:16; cf., Gal. 3:29; Eph. 1:11,14; Phil. 3:3) and considers every believer a Jew, in the spiritual sense of heart circumcision (Rom. 2:29). James also addresses his church letter to "the twelve tribes who are dispersed abroad" (James 1:1; cf., Titus 2:14; 1 Peter 2:9).[2]

Having seen the sealing of those who must endure the im-

---

[1] The figure reflects the practice of oriental kings sealing official documents with their signet rings. By placing the signet of the ring upon something, possession was authenticated and secured (cf., Dan. 6:17; Matt. 27:66). In this picture, the seal gave evidence that the church was under God's authority. Later we learn that the mark upon the saints is the Father's name (14:1; cf., 22:4). By contrast, those who worship the beast bear his mark on their forehead (13:16,17; 14:9,11; 16:2; 19:20; 20:4). A counterpart to the sealing of the church here is the mark of the cross upon the servants of God in Ezekiel 9:4, where those with this sign are promised protection in the coming judgment upon Jerusalem.

[2] Some would limit the 144,000 only to those Christians who will be martyred, appealing especially to 14:4, where 144,000 are said to have been "purchased from among men as first fruits to God and to the Lamb." In this view, the 144,000 might be the completed number of the martyr souls anticipated in 6:9–11. Others identify the number with Israel, taking it, in a literal sense, to mean a full complement of Jews will be saved.

pending upheavals, John has a second vision, which projects the scene of blessing to heaven and anticipates the joy when all the redeemed will be gathered at the throne (7:9–17). They are not bruised and threadbare from the struggles out of which they have come, but like the elders and martyrs before them, these saints are clothed in clean, white robes of victory. Whether or not they have given their bodies in physical martyrdom, they have all shared the spiritual reality of offering their bodies as living sacrifices unto God. Holding palm branches indicative of triumphant joy, they laud and magnify Him who has won the victory—not through force of arms, as kings of the earth, but by giving Himself to die for the world.

Standing about the throne with the living creatures, the elders, and the angels, the multitude is so vast that the number cannot be counted. It streams forth in every direction, as far as the eye can see. Just as God promised to Abraham, it is numberless as the stars of heaven (Gen. 15:5) and the sands of the seashore (Gen. 32:12). "From every nation and all tribes and peoples and tongues" (7:9), the redeemed are gathered.[3] All the servants of God, from the foundation of the world, great and small, young and old, are there before the Lamb.

### The Salvation Shout

With a loud voice, the multitude cries, "Salvation to our God who sits on the throne, and to the Lamb" (7:10). An expanded paraphrase might read: "Thou, our God, sitting in majesty and power upon Thy throne, together with the Lamb who died in our place, are the cause and the means of our salvation. Without Thy effectual calling and care, and the

---

[3] This fourfold description, symbolic of universality, already noted in 5:9, occurs again in 11:9, 13:7, 14:6, and in a modified form of one member in 10:11 and 17:15. It will be observed that the order differs in each instance.

blood of Thy Son, we could not have triumphed over evil or entered into Thy presence adorned in holiness. It is all Thy doing, and to Thee belongs all the glory."

Observe that salvation is ascribed to God, for in reality, the whole work of redemption is initiated and sustained by divine grace (cf., Luke 3:6; Acts 28:28; Titus 2:11). Whether it be the celestial hosts in heaven or the ransomed souls from earth, no one can come into the presence of the Almighty except by His prevenance. The acclamation acknowledges the creature's dependence and gratitude, while also conveying a collective feeling of personal possession—He that sits upon the throne is *our* God.

The recognition of the Lamb accents again the atoning sacrifice of the Son; a truth amplified later by an elder, explaining the beautiful apparel of the multitude: "They have washed their robes and made them white in the blood of the Lamb" (7:14). Both verbs are in the past tense (aorist), which underscores the accomplished work of Christ on their behalf: Every provision has been made for His people to be thoroughly cleansed. Deliverance from sin and its effect is complete.

This blood-washed throng about the throne brings to mind the children of Israel, who washed their clothes in preparation for God's appearance on Mount Sinai (Ex. 19:10–14). The outward cleansing of their garments was a visible token of their inward sanctification. Still, on that occasion, so awesome was God's holiness—His utter separateness from anything defiled—that the Israelites could not come near the mount, upon pain of death. What a contrast to the scene in heaven, where the multitudes, as a holy priesthood, in full assurance of faith, have boldness to enter into the very Holy of Holies (cf., Heb. 10:10–22).

There they serve God "day and night" in His sanctuary, indicating the unceasing nature of heavenly activity. "And He who sits on the throne shall spread His tabernacle over them" (7:15); or it might be translated, "He will make His Shechinah to dwell with them."[4] The reference awakens memories of the tabernacle in the wilderness, where God would visibly demonstrate His glory in the sight of all Israel (Lev. 26:11,12; cf., Ex. 40:34–38; 2 Chron. 7:1–3). In its larger sense, the overshadowing heavenly Shechinah is the fulfillment of the promise that God would forever dwell in the midst of His people (e.g., Isa. 4:5,6; Ezk. 37:27; Zech. 2:10).

Salvation introduces them to a new life of blessedness. Never again will they suffer from the ravages of nature. "They shall hunger no more, neither thirst any more," something especially meaningful to persons who have lived in a land where both food and water were always scarce, even more so for those persecuted for righteousness' sake (7:16). The harassed Christians, many of whom had been driven into desolate wastelands for shelter, would also appreciate the promise that never again would the sun of the desert beat upon them, or any scorching heat (7:16; cf., Isa. 49:10). In a deeper spiritual sense, the longings of the soul will be satisfied, and those that hunger and thirst after righteousness shall be filled (cf., Matt. 5:6). As Jesus said, ". . . he who comes to Me shall not hunger, and he who believes in Me shall never thirst" (John 6:35).

Highlighting this state of continual happiness, "the Lamb in the center of the throne shall be their shepherd, and shall guide them to springs of the water of life . . ." (7:17). The metaphor incorporates a familiar theme throughout Scripture, in which God is likened to a Shepherd who comes for His flock (Isa. 40:11; Psa. 23:1), and also Jesus' picture of Himself as the Good Shepherd, who gives His life for the sheep (John 10:1–30; cf., John 21:15–17; 1 John 3:16; Ezk. 34:23). The Shepherd-Lamb will lead His people to the fountainhead of life, where in the divine Presence they shall know

---

[4] Leon Morris, *The Revelation of St. John* (Grand Rapids: Wm. B. Eerdmans, 1969), p. 118.

fullness of joy and pleasures forevermore (cf., Psa. 36:8,9; Isa.
12:3; John 4:14; John 7:38).

Such life is too wonderful to describe. So great is its gladness, so unspeakable its consolation, that the emotions of the
saints can only be expressed in tears of joy. Whereupon God,
knowing the insufficiency of language to convey the feelings
of love, with infinite understanding, "shall wipe every tear
from their eyes" (7:17). Or this may indicate that memories of
old disappointments and sorrows will be erased from their
minds.

## A Festival of Thanksgiving

There is much in this scene that is reminiscent of the Feast
of the Tabernacles, that joyous holiday at the end of the harvest season for giving thanks for the ingathering of the fruits,
while also commemorating the miraculous interposition of
God tabernacling with, or over, His people when He brought
them through the desert, into the promised land (Ex. 23:16;
Ex. 34:22; Lev. 23:33–43; Num. 29:12–39; Deut. 16:13–17).
In its prophetic spiritual significance, the feast also pointed
to the completed harvest in the end time, when God would
gather His own from "all nations, swallow up death for all
time," and "wipe tears away from all faces" (Isa. 25:7,8; cf.,
Zech. 14:16–21). Its observance was marked by such gladness
that the rabbis said, "He who has not seen its joys knows not
what joy is."[5]

The feast lasted a week, with a special ceremony on the
final day.[6] During this time, the Israelites lived in booths that

---

[5] Quoted in David Smith, *The Days of His Flesh* (New York: Harper),
p. 330.

[6] Information about the observance of this feast can be found in any
Bible dictionary. However, for a comprehensive description, I know of
none better than Alfred Edersheim's, *The Temple, Its Ministry and Ser-
vices* (London: Religious Tract Society, 1874), pp. 232–249.

they made out of tree twigs, intertwined with olive and myr-
tle, reminding them of their pilgrim sojourn on the earth.
Every day, an abundance of offerings was brought to the altar
and sacrificed unto the Lord. While the morning sacrifice was
being prepared, a priest, accompanied by a singing procession bearing palm branches, went down to the pool of Si-
loam, where he drew water into a golden pitcher (cf., Isa.
12:3). Returning to the temple as his brethren conveyed the
sacrifice to the altar, amid a blare of trumpets, he poured the
water into a silver basin in the courtyard. Note how the proceeding with the water was interlocked with the sacrifice, for
no blessing can ever be given, except through the blood of
Christ.

As soon as the vessel was emptied, the Levites lifted their
voices and began to sing the "Hallel," Psalms 113–118. When
the choir came to the words "Give thanks to the Lord" (Psa.
118:1), all the people joined in and waved their palm
branches toward the altar. This was repeated at another
point in Psalms 118:25, and again at the close, as the words
rang out, "Give thanks to the Lord" (Psa. 118:29).[7] Though
the ritual gave thanks for the showers wherewith God had
given the harvest of the fields, the real spiritual reference was
to the future outpouring of the Holy Spirit, when God would
interpose His blessing upon all peoples.[8]

It was on the last day of this feast, after the priest had
poured out the contents of the golden pitcher and the choir
had sung the "Hallel" while the people responded with
praises—when the excitement of the crowd had reached its

---

[7] This has bearing on the significance of the people waving their palm
branches and shouting "Hosanna" when Jesus came the last time into
Jerusalem. However veiled, it was an act of identifying Him with the
anticipated salvation of the nations through the Son of David.

[8] Supporting this future reference, according to the Talmud, the seventy bullocks offered in sacrifice on the last day of the feast were meant
"to correspond to the number of the seventy nations in the world."
Edersheim, op. cit., p. 240.

highest pitch—that the voice of Jesus was heard among the startled multitudes: "If any man is thirsty, let him come to Me and drink. He who believes in Me, as the Scripture said, 'From his innermost being shall flow rivers of living water'" (John 7:37,38; cf., John 7:2; Isa. 44:3; Isa. 55:1; Isa. 58:11). This He spoke of the Spirit whom those that believed on Him were to receive (John 7:39). We can understand the consternation that His declaration provoked among the masses and why, especially among the priests and Pharisees, it was greeted with hostility. As He had said, one had to believe on Him, to know the reality of His words, and this they were unwilling to do. But for those who come to Him and drink from the fountain of living water, the thirst of the soul is quenched forever.

All that was portrayed in the Feast of the Tabernacles thus finds fruition in Christ, and it will be celebrated by all nations, when the palm-bearing multitude assembles at the throne of heaven and sings the song of salvation. At last the harvest will be gathered; the wanderings of His people will be ended; and the long-awaited rejoicing in the land of promise will come to blessed realization.

Sing we the song of those who stand
  Around the eternal throne,
Of every kindred, clime, and land—
  A multitude unknown.

Life's poor distinctions vanish here;
  Today the young, the old,
Our Saviour and His flock, appear,
  One Shepherd and one flock.

Toil, trial, suff'ring, still await
  On earth the pilgrim throng;
Yet learn we in our low estate
  The church triumphant song.

Then hallelujah! power and praise
To God in Christ be given;
May all who now this anthem raise,
Renew the song in heaven.

JAMES MONTGOMERY

# 8

# *The Antiphonal Amen*

"Amen, blessing and glory and wisdom and thanksgiving and honor and power and might, be to our God forever and ever. Amen."

REVELATION 7:12

## Angels on Their Faces

A soldier, captured during a battle of the Civil War, was brought to Richmond for confinement in Libby Prison. As he waited for the heavy gates to open, his heart filled with fear at the thought of the suffering which was to be his on the other side of the walls.

Just then, a chaplain records, a low voice sang out from an upper window: "Praise God, from whom all blessings flow."

Several more voices joined him in the second line: "Praise Him, all creatures here below."

By this time, scores of men lifted the words: "Praise Him above, ye heavenly host."

And then, as the last line was reached, it seemed the whole prison responded with the doxology: "Praise Father, Son, and Holy Ghost."[1]

Many persons have had similar experiences. Praise is contagious. Certainly it is manifest among the hosts about the

---

[1] The printed excerpt from which this story was taken came out of a periodical near the turn of the century, but regretfully, I cannot locate the name or date. As to the doxology, it was written by Bishop Thomas Ken of England, sometime in the seventeenth century. It has become the most familiar of all Protestant affirmations of praise.

throne, as the adoration of one group stirs another to join the heavenly choir. The pattern suggests a spontaneous antiphonal reaction.

No sooner has the last line of the multitude's chorus echoed through the celestial habitation, than the myriad hosts of angels pick up the song. They are standing around the throne, the elders, and the four living creatures, but when the saved ones declare their thanks, the angels prostrate themselves before the throne and worship God. The intensity of their homage may be felt in the expression, ". . . they fell on their faces," conveying an even stronger sense of devotion.

In the former scene in which the angels offer adoration (5:12), the Lamb is the object of their praise. Here it is specifically God, sitting upon the throne, who receives their reverence. The blood-washed ones attributed salvation to their God, yet He is equally the God of the angels. And, as has already been noted, they have a special fascination with the saving work of Christ. To behold now these witnesses—who have been brought out of great trials—standing before the throne, invokes indescribable joy. If angels rejoice over just one sinner who repents (Luke 15:10), how much more must they celebrate when the whole ransomed church of God comes into its inheritance.

I recall once talking with a mother who told me that she heard angels singing when her little boy died. This was easy for me to believe. Not that angels will be heard every time a child dies, but if children have angels who behold the face of their Father (Matt. 18:3,10), why should it seem strange to hear them singing when the veil between earth and heaven is rent at death?

One of the angels' ministries is to escort the soul of a righteous pilgrim into God's Presence, when it is separated from the body (Luke 16:22). I recall the late Harold Paul Sloan, a beloved Methodist pastor in Philadelphia, telling about the death of his mother. Because of the nature of her condition during the last months of her illness, she could not lie down on the bed, but was confined to a wheelchair, where she required constant attendance. Dr. Sloan was with her during the last hours. As she died, he said, it seemed that another person entered the room. He started to turn around, to see who it was, when suddenly his mother rose completely out of the chair, lifted her hands in the air, and shouted the praises of God. Then her limp body fell back into the wheelchair, but her free spirit was taken by the unseen angel into the bosom of Abraham.

In the larger context of the end times in the gathering of the church, the angels are directly involved. They are God's reapers of the harvest (Matt. 13:39). At the trumpet sound, ". . . they will gather together His elect from the four winds, from one end of the sky to the other" (Matt. 24:31), even as they sever the just from the wicked (Matt. 13:41,49,50). And in heaven, Jesus will confess His witnesses before the angels (Luke 12:8; cf., Luke 20:35,36; Matt. 22:30). They are His worshiping host (Heb. 1:6).

## So Be It

We are not surprised when the angels cry, "Amen," expressing their full agreement with the gratitude of the victorious multitude (7:12; cf., 5:14). The word *amen* means to affirm that which is certain or reliable, that which can be trusted without question.[2] It was a common practice in the church, as in Jewish synagogues, to voice this accent after hearing a thanksgiving or an important truth (e.g., 1:7; 22:17; 1 Cor. 14:16; Rom. 15:33; Gal. 6:18). By saying *amen*, one not only expressed agreement with the statement of another, but also made it binding on himself.

---

[2] The word occurs 126 times in the New Testament, 100 of them in the Gospels, from the mouth of Jesus. A good summary of the use of this term, both in the Old and New Testaments, is in Colin Brown, ed., *The New International Dictionary of New Testament Theology* I (Grand Rapids: Zondervan, 1977), pp. 97–99.

In contrast to the prevailing custom today, Jesus often introduced His own words with the word *amen* or "truly, I say to you" (e.g., Matt. 6:2,5,16; Matt. 8:10; Matt. 10:23; Matt. 19:28; Matt. 24:34; Matt. 25:40 al.), sometimes even doubling the amen (e.g., John 1:51; John 3:3,5,11; John 5:19 al.). Such self-affirmation of the truthfulness of His message was a majestic expression of His authority. *Amen* may be found in other New Testament writings at the close of prayers and doxologies, strengthening their force (Rom. 1:25; Rom. 9:5; Rom. 11:36; Rom. 16:27; Gal. 1:5; Eph. 3:21; Phil. 4:20; Heb. 13:21). In its highest form, the word is used of Christ Himself (3:14), which echoes Isaiah's reference to the God of the Amen, or truth (Isa. 65:16). Of course, when one thinks of the inspired Word, he realizes that all the promises of God in Christ ". . . are yes; wherefore also by Him is our Amen" (2 Cor. 1:20).

Having confirmed the witness of the church, the angels lift up their own tribute, in the familiar sevenfold doxology emphasizing completeness: "Blessing and glory and wisdom and thanksgiving and honor and power and might, be to our God" (7:12). Six of the seven attributes are the same as those expressed before, though the order is different. A definite article here before each characteristic serves to make the meaning more emphatic.

*Blessing* is a serendipity of happiness, a spontaneous overflow of thanksgiving. As attributed to God, it reflects the wonder of the angels before the triumph of His grace. Whether in creation or redemption, all His works praise Him.

*Glory* speaks of majestic radiance, that effulgence of splendor, which surrounds the Most High.

*Wisdom* is displayed in His infinite comprehension of all things—the way He understands and orders events for the accomplishing of His purposes, particularly in the salvation of His people. Any man who would know the truth must first learn of Him who bore our sins to the cross.

*Thanksgiving* comes to God as the only reasonable response to His goodness. He is the giver of every perfect gift, and apart from His sustaining care, there would be no existence. Ingratitude would be the height of blasphemy.

*Honor* becomes the respect due to His Person. So exalted is His name that at its mention, every knee should bow before Him.

*Power* describes His capacity to perform what is inherent in His nature. Just a word from Him, and it is done. He effortlessly accomplishes His purposes, and none can frustrate His designs.

*Might* is that relentless force by which His will prevails overall, the might by which the universe is upheld.

To these ascriptions of praise, the angels add "forever and ever" (7:12), emphasizing again the eternal character of God. Unlike the passing roles of men, His years are without fail, His dominion without end. Attesting to this fact, the angels conclude their affirmation with another mighty "Amen."

## Safe in the Arms of Jesus

How wonderful it is to be held in the firm grip of the everlasting arms! Here is security. Our salvation is not dependent upon the whimsical notions of well-intentioned men, but upon the oath of Him who is eternal verity; it is fastened, with God's own nail-pierced hand, to the unmovable stake of His incorruptible nature.

Persons with this peace like to sing the Lord's praise, thus invariably creating an atmosphere strangely different from the world. A Finnish officer, serving with the army during the Finnish-Russian War, tells of such an experience, which completely altered the course of his life.[3] After one of the battles,

---

[3] The Finnish officer is only identified by the name of Nordenberg. His story, reported to be true, is taken from John Myers, comp., *Voices From the Edge of Eternity* (Old Tappan: Fleming H. Revell Co., 1971), pp. 219–222.

a number of Red prisoners were placed under his guard, seven of whom were sentenced to be shot at dawn the next day. Confined in a cold basement room, the condemned men, with unrestrained anguish, swore and beat on the walls with their bleeding fists.

However, the officer, standing outside, noticed one prisoner, Koskinen by name, who was different from the rest. While the others raved and cursed, he sat quietly on his bench. Then, after a while, in a wavering voice that grew stronger, he began to sing:

> Safe in the arms of Jesus,
>     Safe on His gentle breast,
> There by His love o'er shaded,
>     Sweetly my soul shall rest.

Over and over he sang the words. When he stopped, a wild-looking man erupted, "Where did you get that, you fool?"

The man looked at his comrades with tear-filled eyes and replied, "You ask me where I got this song. It was from the Salvation Army—I heard it three weeks ago. My mother sang about Jesus and prayed to Him."

He paused a moment, as if to gather courage. Then, rising to his feet and looking straight in front of him, he said, "It is cowardly to hide your beliefs. The God my mother believed in is now my God. As I lay awake, I saw mother's face before me. It reminded me of the song I had heard. I prayed that Christ would forgive me and make me ready to stand before Him. . . . Since then, this verse has been sounding within me. I can no longer keep it to myself."

"You are right," said one comrade. "If only I knew there was mercy for me, too, but I have reviled God and trampled on all that is holy." Sinking to the floor in despair, he groaned, "Pray for me, Koskinen."

The two Red soldiers went down on their knees and prayed for each other. It was no long prayer—but it reached heaven.

A door seemed to open to another world, and everyone sensed the nearness of an unseen hallowed Presence. Before long, all the prisoners were on their faces before God. As they prayed and wept, an indescribable change took place. The Spirit of God filled the room, and the conversation turned to spiritual things—truth hidden from kings and queens, but revealed unto babes.

Occasionally they would break into singing, not only the favorite song of Koskinen, but verses and choruses of others long forgotten. The soldiers on guard united with them, for the power of God had touched them all. The angels must have joined in, too, as Zion's praises resounded through the crisp early-morning air.

At daybreak, as the first rays of light came over the horizon, the condemned men were marched out to the place of execution. Standing before the firing squad, they asked that the usual covering not be placed over their heads and that they be allowed to sing, for one last time, Koskinen's song. Permission was granted. So before the command to fire was given, the seven men lifted their hands to heaven and, with uncovered faces, sang with all their might:

> Safe in the arms of Jesus,
> Safe on His gentle breast,
> There by His love o'er shaded,
> Sweetly my soul shall rest.
> Hark! it's the voice of angels,
> Borne in a song to me,
> Over the fields of jasper,
> Over the crystal sea.

Can you hear them in their joyous witness? Then lift your hands and, with your eyes upon the throne, join the hosts of heaven in a blessed Amen.

> Jesus, my heart's dear Refuge,
> Jesus has died for me.

Firm on the Rock of Ages
　　Ever my trust shall be.
Here let me wait with patience;
　　Wait till the night is o'er;
Wait till I see the morning
　　Break on the golden shore.
Safe in the arms of Jesus,
　　Safe on His gentle breast,
There by His love o'er shaded,
　　Sweetly my soul shall rest.

FANNY CROSBY

# 9

# *The Kingdom Carol*

"The kingdom of the world has become the kingdom of
our Lord, and of His Christ; and He will reign forever
and ever."

REVELATION 11:15

## Reassuring Voices

With the vision of the ultimate salvation of the nations
fresh in mind, the Lamb opens the seventh seal of the book of
destiny, disclosing the final tragic events in the world's history. This new revelation brought "silence in heaven for
about half an hour" (8:1). So fearful are the terrors about to
be unleashed upon the earth that the worshiping hosts
around the throne hush their singing. The stillness serves to
heighten the suspense of the last act of the divine drama to
follow, while it is also expressive of the awe felt, when pon-
dering the day of the Lord (Zeph. 1:7,10; Zech. 2:13; Hab.
2:20).

During this brief pause, seven angels are seen standing before God (8:2). To each is given a trumpet,[1] recalling the

---

[1] The seven trumpets in Revelation, as well as the seven bowls that
follow, are sometimes interpreted chronologically, with each one en-
larging on the seventh element of the previous series; that is, the seven
trumpets expand on the seventh seal, while the seven bowls zero in on
the seventh trumpet. Another point of view regards the seals, trumpets,
and bowls as describing the same events in different ways. Or we may
see in them elements of both these views, believing that there is a general progression, as the judgments move toward the end, but not without

prophecy: "Near is the great day of the Lord . . . . A day of
wrath is that day, a day of trouble and distress, a day of destruction and desolation, a day of darkness and gloom . . . .
a day of trumpet and battle cry . . ." (Zeph. 1:14–16). Before
the trumpets sound, however, another angel, standing over
the altar, is given incense in a golden censer, that he should
add it to the prayers of all the saints going up to God (8:3,4;
cf., 5:8).[2] Then something happens that graphically relates
the intercessions of the saints to God's judgments. The angel
takes the censer, fills it with fire from the altar, and in one
dramatic gesture, casts it upon the earth (cf., Ezk. 10:2–7). It
indicates that these prayers are someway involved in the cul-
mination of history. That God is about to act is seen in the
mighty thunderings, voices, lightnings, and an earthquake
(8:5), while the angels prepare to show what is to come (8:6).

There follows a succession of calamities, as the seven
angels sound their trumpets. The first four, retrospective of
the Egyptian plagues preceding the Exodus, declare judgments upon the physical universe, bringing complete destruction to a third part of the earth (8:7–12). Still, a bird of

---

some recapitulation of details. Whatever view one may hold about this
earthly sequence, the essential meaning of the heavenly songs is not af-
fected. If one desires a good résumé of the different ways to view the
structure of Revelation, see Donald Guthrie, *New Testament Introduc-
tion: Hebrews to Revelation* III (London: Tyndale Press, 1962), pp.
289–296.

[2] The temporal analogy here is to the priests in the temple, daily taking grains of incense and placing them on the golden altar, to make a
sweet-smelling offering to God that would fill the sanctuary with fragrance (Ex. 30:1–10; Heb. 9:4; cf., Luke 1:9; Eph. 5:2). Live coals used to
kindle the incense were taken from the brazen altar of sacrifice outside
the sanctuary and just inside the eastern gate. Here, every morning and
evening, the blood of the substitutionary sacrifice was poured out before
God, and the whole flesh of the animal, symbolical of the total dedication of the people, consumed as an offering of burnt sacrifice. Hence, the
same fire that consumed the sacrifice kindled the incense. Prayer comes
to God by way of the blood.

prey, flying through the sky crying, "Woe, woe, woe," indicates that the worst is yet to come. What is meant by the first two *woes* becomes evident as the fifth and sixth trumpets sound, and horrifying demonic creatures arise from the abyss, to bring torment and death upon the unrepentant inhabitants of the earth (9:1–21).

Before the seventh trumpet sounds, however, another strong angel is seen coming down out of heaven, having open in his hand "a little book" which contains a message for the suffering church in these last days (10:1–11). With awesome authority, the angel announces that "there shall be delay no longer" in the final triumph of God over evil (10:6) and that, within the period of the seventh trumpet, the mystery of the kingdom of God will be disclosed (10:7). Realizing that the church will come into her glory is sweet to the taste, but knowing that the event will be preceded by terrible satanic opposition is bitter to swallow (10:8–10). The extent of that persecution to come is depicted by two witnesses, characteristic of Moses and Elijah, who faithfully proclaim the Word of God, until killed by the powers of Antichrist that enslave the world (11:3–10). Their bodies are left unburied in the streets, symbolic of the disdain of the church by society in the last day. But the reveling of wicked men suddenly ends, as the martyred witnesses are resurrected and taken up into heaven (11:11–13). This visible rapture, together with a mighty earthquake, compels the masses to recognize that God is sovereign. The first two woes have now passed, but before the third is described (11:14), as the last trumpet sounds, we have another glimpse at the throne of God.

"Loud voices" are heard in heaven, declaring the certainty of God's eternal reign. Though the identity of these voices is not specified, they seem to speak for celestial beings whose relationship to Christ is more distant than that enjoyed by the redeemed.

**The Reign of Christ**

With symphonic delight, they cry, "The kingdom of the world has become the kingdom of our Lord, and of His Christ; and He will reign forever and ever" (11:15). The contest is not for the varying political systems of the world, as might be inferred if there were a number of kingdoms[3]; rather, the issue is the singular allegiance of the world system itself. Satan was willing to give Jesus the kingdoms of the earth, in exchange for His homage, but worship by the inhabitants of the world, he still intended for himself (Matt. 4:8–10; Luke 4:5–8).

The essence of the declaration is that the rule of this world has passed into the hands of the rightful King. Actually, sovereignty has always been with God and His Anointed, even though satanic forces in this world have appeared to be in charge. But the demonic conspiracy that infiltrates and seeks to govern all the institutions of man is neither invincible nor permanent. In the manifestation of the Lord from heaven, the pretentious reign of the usurper will be revealed for what it is, and God will assert His kingly power over the rebellious earth.

The promise of the kingdom—God's reign over His people—runs throughout Scripture. Inherently, of course, God is King over all the earth (2 Kings 19:15; Isa. 6:5; Jer. 46:18; Psa. 29:10; Psa. 47:2; Psa. 99:1–4; Psa. 145:11). But in a still more special way, He is King of Israel, working in its history to show His glory (Ex. 15:17,18; Deut. 33:5; Isa. 43:15). Even though His kingdom was never fully realized in experience, the children of Abraham lived in the promise of a messianic age, when their King would rule over all nations. However misunderstood the spiritual dimension of this faith may have

---

[3] The familiar King James Version, following some codices, renders this phrase in the plural, "the kingdoms." However, most manuscripts have the singular, as noted here.

been, the promise of the coming King was there, to give them hope and joy during the toilsome journeys of this world.

It was seen as a day when "the God of heaven will set up a kingdom which will never be destroyed," a kingdom that "will crush and put an end" to all the kingdoms of men (Dan. 2:44; cf., Dan. 2:31–45; Dan. 4:3,34; Dan. 6:26). In that time, "the Lord will be king over all the earth" (Zech. 14:9), and "there will be no end to the increase of His government or of peace" (Isa. 9:7; cf., Micah 4:7). This age was to be inaugurated with the coming of "the Son of Man" in the clouds of heaven, when there would be given to Him "dominion, glory, and a kingdom . . . which will not pass away" nor ever be destroyed (Dan. 7:13,14). Likewise, "the saints of the Highest One," comprising "all the peoples, nations, and men of every language," will receive the kingdom with their King, and they will serve and obey Him forever (Dan. 7:18,14,22,25,27).

Jesus saw the fulfillment of this promise in His life and work. Again and again, He spoke of Himself as the Son of Man,[4] declaring not only His identity with the coming kingdom, but affirming that, in Him, it was a present reality. His first coming into the world, to die as the sacrificial Lamb, was never isolated in His mind from His Second Coming as the triumphant King. As He went about doing good, He announced that the kingdom was at hand (Matt. 4:17,23; Mark 1:15; Luke 4:43). What did it matter, that He was despised and rejected by the world? The Son of Man someday was coming in the glory of the kingdom, to take His place at the right hand of power, and all the enemies of God would be put under His feet (Matt. 16:27; Matt. 24:30; Matt. 25:31;

---

[4] There are eight-two references to this title in the words of Jesus, which is more than of any other self-designation in the Gospels. For a discussion of this whole concept, see Robert E. Coleman, "His Heavenly Vision," *The Mind of the Master* (Old Tappan: Fleming H. Revell Co., 1977), pp. 102–118. In this work, many other sources are cited for further study.

Mark 8:38; Mark 13:26; Luke 9:26; Luke 21:27). The victory shouts about the throne were already vibrant in His soul.

Those who believed on Him learned to live in this same consciousness (Luke 17:20,21; John 3:3,5). They preached the good news of the kingdom (Matt. 10:7,8; Luke 9:2; Luke 10:9); as inheritors of the kingdom, they ministered to the hungry, the sick, the naked, the imprisoned, and the stranger (Matt. 25:34–40); they prayed for the coming of the kingdom (Matt. 6:10; Luke 11:2); whether eating or drinking, working or playing, the kingdom was ever before them (Matt. 6:33; Luke 12:31,32). Whatever their lot in this world, they knew that the King of heaven reigned in their hearts and that, by His grace, someday they would reign with Him in glory (Matt. 19:17; Matt. 25:34).

## Our Coming King

With such assurance, we need have no fear of the future. A Christian nurse once asked a soldier, dying of wounds in an army hospital, if he was prepared for death. The large, dark eyes of the youth opened, a smile came over his face, and he answered, "I am ready, dear lady, for this has been His kingdom." As he spoke, he placed his hand over his breast. When the boy died, not long afterward, his hand still lay over his heart.[5]

Because the kingdom is entered now by faith in Christ, nothing else seems so relevant as a witness to the world about that faith. It is this activity, more than anything else, which prepares the way for the King to return. Jesus said, "This gospel of the kingdom shall be preached in the whole world for a witness to all the nations, and then the end shall come"

---

[5] Told by L. B. Balliett, M.D., as recorded by S. B. Shaw, *Dying Testimonies,* and quoted by John Meyers, comp., *Voices From the Edge of Eternity* (Old Tappan: Fleming H. Revell Co., 1971), p. 123.

(Matt. 24:14; cf., Mark 13:10).[6] Since knowledge of the saving Word of Christ actually constitutes "the keys to the kingdom" (Matt. 16:19; cf., Matt. 18:18; John 20:23),[7] possessors of this truth must be faithful in getting out the message to every creature. Time is of the essence. "We have all eternity to celebrate the victories," as Amy Carmichael reminds us, "but only a few hours before sunset to win them."[8]

When we encounter opposition, as surely we will, the inevitable day of the kingdom triumph is reassuring. Such was the case with members of the early church, as they were harassed for their witness. Using the same frame of reference as the heavenly song, they prayed, in the words of the Psalmist, "Why did the Gentiles rage, and the peoples devise futile things?" noting that the kings and rulers of the earth were "gathered together against the Lord, and against His Christ" (Acts 4:25,26; Psa. 2:1,2). But the Christians knew, too, that "He who sits in the heavens laughs" at the futile efforts of this world's powers to defeat His purposes (Psa. 2:4). The things that happened to God's Anointed were according to His determinate counsel (Acts 4:27,28), and His people were confident that He would undertake by His Spirit, as He had bidden them to pray. God had promised to give them the nations for their inheritance and the very ends of the earth as their possession (Psa. 2:8).

---

[6] As might be expected, there are different ways in which presenting the Gospel witness is interpreted as fulfilling this mandate. Some see its realization in worldwide radio broadcasts. Others point out the necessity of translating and preaching the message into the native tongues of all groups, before communication has been effected. And, in a very general sense, there are those who believe that the Gospel has already been conveyed to all nations, citing such references as Colossians 1:5,6 and Acts 8:4.

[7] The effect of this statement is that belief in the saving truth, as taught by Christ and entrusted to the disciples, would be ratified in heaven. For a discussion of this passage, see my note in *The Mind of the Master*, op. cit., p. 112.

[8] Amy Carmichael, quoted in *Decision*, June 1963, p. 13.

Here we catch again the fulfillment of the kingdom hope, as the Scripture had promised: "All the ends of the earth will remember and turn to the Lord, And all the families of the nations will worship before" Him. "For the kingdom is the Lord's, And He rules over the nations" (Psa. 22:27,28; cf., Psa. 96:3,10; Isa. 2:2; Isa. 11:9).

What a thrill, to live in this certainty! Disciples will be made of all nations. Though the work be hard, the end will justify every sacrifice. Tears shed on earth will be pearls in heaven. They that go forth with weeping, carrying the seed of the Gospel, "Shall indeed come again with a shout of joy," bringing their sheaves with them (Psa. 126:6).

Reverend E. P. Scott, a pioneer missionary to India, in one of his journeys to an unreached area, came upon a savage band on a war expedition. They seized him and pointed their spears at his heart. Feeling utterly helpless, not knowing what else to do, he drew out the violin he always carried with him and began to play and sing, in the native language: "All hail the power of Jesus' name."

As the music and words of the song rang out, he closed his eyes, expecting death at any moment. But when nothing happened, even after the third stanza, he opened his eyes and was amazed to see that the spears had fallen from the hands of his captors and tears filled their eyes. They invited him to their homes, and for several years he labored among them, winning many to Christ.[9]

I like to think of this experience as a parable of the coming kingdom. Those who bring the good tidings may not always be delivered from the spears of the enemy. Nevertheless, the name of Christ will someday prevail to the ends of the earth, and He shall be crowned Lord of all!

---

[9] Louis Albert Banks, *Immortal Hymns and Their Stories* (Cleveland: Burrows Brothers, 1898), pp. 312, 313; *see also* Amos R. Wells, "All Hail the Power of Jesus' Name," *The Christian Endeavor World*, May 26, 1904.

All hail the power of Jesus' name!
   Let angels prostrate fall;
Bring forth the royal diadem,
   And crown him Lord of all.

Ye chosen seed of Israel's race,
   Ye ransom'd from the fall,
Hail him who saves you by his grace,
   And crown him Lord of all.

Sinners, whose love can ne'er forget
   The wormwood and the gall,
Go spread your trophies at his feet,
   And crown him Lord of all.

Let every kindred, every tribe,
   On this terrestrial ball,
To him all majesty ascribe,
   And crown him Lord of all.

O that with yonder sacred throng
   We at his feet may fall!
We'll join the everlasting song,
   And crown him Lord of all.

                    EDWARD PERRONET

# 10

# The Psalm of Judgment

"We give Thee thanks, O Lord God, the Almighty, who art and who wast, because Thou has taken Thy great power and hast begun to reign. And the nations were enraged, and Thy wrath came, and the time came for the dead to be judged, and the time to give their reward to Thy bond-servants the prophets and to the saints and to those who fear Thy name, the small and the great, and to destroy those who destroy the earth."

REVELATION 11:17,18

## Recognition of Power

A Soviet exhibition in New York featured a picture of Lenin that towered over the display, with the caption: "All power in the Soviet Union belongs to the working people of town and country."

Those who see no higher authority than man naturally locate power in some form of totalitarian control, usually resident in the state. Such absolutizing of sinful man invariably leads to human degradation, and finally, moral tyranny. There must be an authority above man, a fixed standard of perfection, if there is to be justice and liberty. True human dignity comes only in loving submission to Him who said, "All authority has been given to Me in heaven and on earth" (Matt. 28:18).

This truth is dramatically illustrated again in "the twenty-four elders, who sit on their thrones before God," indicative of their honored position of dominion (11:16). As the song of the kingdom reverberates through heaven, these celestial representatives of the redeemed cannot remain in their royal seats, but—characteristic of their deference to higher authority—"fell on their faces and worshiped God" (11:16; cf., 4:4,10; 5:8,14; 7:11; 19:4). The double verbs of devotion here underscore the proper attitude of every created being in the divine Presence. In this adoring homage, their voices continue the laudation of the King.

## Gratitude for Judgment

It is a hymn of thanksgiving to the omnipotent Sovereign who has, with mighty power, taken charge of the situation. "We give Thee thanks, O Lord God, the Almighty, who art and who wast . . ." (11:17; cf., 4:8).[1] The repeated affirmation of the divine name is especially fitting in this context, where the judgment of contending forces is celebrated. Also, the title appropriately stresses the immutable and eternal nature of God's decrees—He is the everlasting Contemporary, the One who never changes, whose will is inviolable.

The long mystery of God's rule is now revealed; that which has been hidden from the ages is manifest to all: "Thou hast taken Thy great power and hast begun to reign" (11:17). The verb forms here, as elsewhere in the song, emphasize the certainty of what is at hand. "Thou hast taken" is a perfect tense, indicating an act which continues on into the future. It assures that the dethronement of evil is permanent. The other verb "has begun" is in the aorist tense, which means that His triumph is decisive; it is accomplished. As far as God's design is concerned, the King has already taken to Himself His great power and entered upon His reign.

---

[1] The King James Version adds the phrase, "which art to come," found in some manuscripts. Actually it would seem superfluous in this setting, since the kingdom has already come.

Like the host before them, the elders then draw upon the Second Psalm in speaking of God's wrath upon the rebellious earth. "And the nations were enraged, and Thy wrath came, and the time came for the dead to be judged" (11:18; cf., Psa. 2:5,12; Joel 3:9–13; Zech. 14:2–4). What is implied in this judgment is depicted in subsequent chapters, culminating in the final sentencing by Him who sits on the great, white throne, "from whose presence earth and heaven fled away" (20:11). All who have ever lived will be gathered there, their bodies raised and joined with their spirits; from cemeteries in hills and valleys, from the ocean depths, from battlefields long forgotten, they will come—"the dead, the great and the small," and will stand "before the throne." Then the books will be opened, along with the book of life, and the dead will be judged "from the things which were written in the books, according to their deeds" (20:12,13).

For the unbeliever and apostate, of course, it will be a time of fearful retribution, for whoever is not found in the book of life will be cast into the lake of fire. "This is the second death" (20:14,15).

We can understand why "the nations were enraged" (11:18). Judgment, for those who forget God, is frightening to imagine. No wonder that, at the prospect of judgment, the wicked cry for the mountains and rocks to fall upon them and hide them from the face of Him who sits upon the throne (6:16,17). Yet the day of reckoning cannot be escaped. All "the cowardly and unbelieving and abominable and murderers and immoral persons and sorcerers and idolaters and all liars" shall be turned into hell (21:8; cf., 21:27; 22:15), a place of unending torment, prepared for the devil and his demons, "where decay never stops and the fire never goes out" (Mark 9:48 PHILLIPS; cf., Matt. 8:12; Matt. 13:42, 50; Matt. 22:13; Matt. 24:51; Matt. 25:30, 41; Luke 16:23, 28). Every recourse of mercy is gone. These evil persons are left in the terrifying loneliness of "outer darkness" forever (Matt. 8:12; Matt. 22:13; Matt. 25:30).

Let it be clear that this judgment is determined by God, not by His creatures. Though Spirit-led prayers enter into the processes of history leading up to this day, and there is a sense in which the saints assist in this judgment of the world (cf., 1 Cor. 6:2), still the execution of justice is decided by Him who sits on the throne. I cannot help but think that much anguish in this life could be avoided, if we would keep this in mind.

Judgment, however, does not only concern the ungodly; there is also the judgment of the righteous, which is seen in this reference: "the time to give their reward to Thy bond-servants the prophets and to the saints and to those that fear Thy name, the small and the great" (11:18).[2] Judgment, for the faithful, is not to determine salvation. That has already been settled. This is a judgment of works, when God will "bring to light the things hidden in the darkness and disclose the motives of men's hearts; and then each man's praise will come to him from God" (1 Cor. 4:5). These works will be tried as in the crucible of God's flaming presence, and "the fire itself will test the quality of each man's work" (1 Cor. 3:13). That which has been done with no other motive than to please God will be seen for what it is, and like pure, re-fined metal, endure with reward. By the same criterion, whatever has been done for self-glory will be burned up, the person will suffer loss, "but he himself shall be saved" (1 Cor. 3:15). For, finally, salvation is not earned by works of righteousness of our own; it is received by believing on the finished work of Jesus Christ on our behalf (Eph. 2:8,9). Nevertheless, in accepting His gift, we start working for God, not out of a sense of mere duty, but as a service of love. Men will see these good works and give glory to the Father in heaven

---

[2] In point of time, this judgment of the Christian may precede the final judgment at the great, white throne, depending upon how the millennium is interpreted. The exact chronology and location of this event is immaterial to the song.

(Matt. 5:16). He gets the credit for it, but someday the workers will get a reward (cf., Eph. 6:7,8; Col. 3:24).[3] The crowns of the elders spoke of this idea (4:4,10), and in a more general sense, it is seen in the inheritance of the new Jerusalem.

What a joy this judgment gives to those who want only God to be glorified! For it is certain that, in the end, nothing else will remain. In knowing His exaltation, too, the redeemed can rejoice in their own glorification. Whatever the suffering encountered in this present time, it cannot be compared with the glory that is to be revealed in them (Rom. 8:18; cf., Matt. 5:11,12; 2 Tim. 2:12; Heb. 10:34; Heb. 11:26). The manifestation of every person's work is also a strong incentive to keep pressing the claims of the kingdom, for we must all give account for the deeds done in the flesh. And to whom much is given, much is required (Luke 12:48).

The hymn closes on a somber note, indicating that the time has come "to destroy those who destroy the earth" (11:18). It is a way of saying again that punishment is meted out according to the nature of the offense.[4] Those who have been

---

[3] The future judgment thus relates to the way God's grace is now utilized in fulfilling His calling. There is in this a suggestion that there will be degrees of reward, based on the potential service desired by God, both for the unbeliever and the saved. Some passages which the Christian will find especially revealing, in addition to those cited above, include Matt. 6:1–6; Matt. 10:41,42; Matt. 16:27; Luke 6:35; Rom. 2:10; 1 Cor. 9:17,18; Phil. 4:1; 1 Thess. 2:19; 2 Tim. 4:8; Heb. 11:6; James 1:12; 1 Peter 5:4; 2 John 8; Daniel 12:3.

[4] The Scriptures teach that the measure of revealed truth granted to men will determine the standard by which they are judged. Allowance is made for varying degrees of privilege, both of opportunity and responsibility (Matt. 10:15; Matt. 11:24; John 19:11; Luke 12:48). Persons who have never heard of Christ have the natural law preserved in their conscience and tradition, however obscured and corrupted it may be, to make them accountable (Rom. 1:18–28; Rom. 2:12–15). The Jews have the added instruction of their Scriptures, which not only make clear the absolute standard of perfection under the law, but also point to Christ as Saviour and Messiah (John 5:39–47; John 12:48). Those who have a

unmerciful in their rampage across the earth can expect God's wrath in kind. There is nothing capricious about the righteousness of the Most High.

## Love and Judgment

What follows in the next verse is a confirmation of the elders' song. The temple opens in heaven, and John sees, within, the prototype of the Ark of the Covenant. The exposed Ark comes as a reassurance to the believing community, not only of access to God's immediate Presence, but also of His faithfulness in fulfilling His Word. In the midst of this vision, there appear violent agitations in the cosmos, "flashes of lightning and sounds and peals of thunder and an earthquake and a great hailstorm" (11:19), symbols of God's awesome might in the judgments to come (cf., 8:5; 16:18; 6:12; 8:7; 11:13; 16:21). We are reminded that the blessing and the curse issue from the same throne; God's holy wrath is but the other side of His covenant grace.

In a day of moral flabbiness, when people tend to ignore God's anger against sin, it is easy to confuse this truth. We could learn a great deal from those elders in heaven, who have better vision of reality. They would teach us that God's character being what it is, He must judge that which is an affront to His name. Justice requires that the Lord of all the earth uphold the law of His own righteousness, else His sovereignty would be called into question and His integrity impugned. So necessary is judgment upon sin that in effecting our redemption, He could not spare His own Son, when He

---

knowledge of the Gospel, and who have rejected the light, come under the most severe judgment, "since they again crucify to themselves the Son of God, and put Him to an open shame" (Heb. 6:6; cf., Heb. 10:26–29). In every case, the principle is that the greater degree of privilege brings the greater degree of responsibility before God. Man must give an exact accounting for every bit of truth revealed (e.g., Prov. 1:24–31; Jer. 7:12–16; 2 Thess. 2:10–12).

took upon Himself the iniquity of us all. It is this nature that
blazes against everything which would destroy His beloved.
God loves us too much, to let us live undisturbed in rebellion
and thereby miss His purpose for our lives. That is why He
cast rebellious man out of the garden and brought death upon
the race. It was a merciful way of limiting the extent of corruption, while also teaching us to seek that kingdom over
which death has no rule. If we could but see, all God's judgments in this present world work for the completion of His
redemptive plan, calling us to a more perfect way. Those
who respond with repentance and greater devotion see His
judgments as an act of love and kiss the rod.

On the other hand, those who scorn the Lord see His judgments with trembling discomfort and disdain. Even in hell,
they gnash their teeth in unrepentant remorse. Having
turned their backs upon the love of God, trampling underfoot
the blood of the holy covenant, they must live to themselves
in bitter tears and in unending night.

One might wonder why the elders would be singing about
this day of judgment, realizing that it would mean the final
separation of all who have turned to their own ways. Certainly God has no pleasure in the reprobation of the wicked.
An understanding of their joy, then, lies not in the punishment of the ungodly, but in the triumph of their Lord. The
judgment furnishes a worthy display of His invincible power,
vindicating truth and justice and the honor of His Son. This is
the delight of heaven that finds expression in ceaseless praise.

> Day of judgment! Day of wonders!
>     Hark! the trumpet's awful sound!
> Louder than a thousand thunders,
>     Shakes the vast creation round!
>         How the summons
>     Will the sinner's heart confound!
>
> See the Judge, our nature wearing,
>     Clothed in majesty divine!

Ye who long for His appearing
    Then shall say: "This God is mine!"
        Gracious Saviour,
    Own us in that day as Thine.

At His call, the dead awaken,
    Rise to life from earth and sea;
All the powers of nature, shaken
    By His looks, prepare to see:
        Careless sinner:
    What will then become of thee?

But to those who have confessed,
    Loved and served the Lord below,
He will say: Come near, ye blessed,
    See the Kingdom I bestow.
        You forever
Shall My love and glory know!

JOHN NEWTON

# 11

# The Shout of the Overcomers

"Now the salvation, and the power, and the kingdom of our God and the authority of His Christ have come, for the accuser of our brethren has been thrown down, who accuses them before our God day and night. And they overcame him because of the blood of the Lamb and because of the word of their testimony, and they did not love their life even to death. For this reason, rejoice, O heavens and you who dwell in them. Woe to the earth and the sea; because the devil has come down to you, having great wrath, knowing that he has only a short time."

REVELATION 12:10–12

## Satanic Assault

The early Methodists on the frontier liked to sing, at camp-meeting time, a song celebrating Satan's defeat. Each of the eighteen stanzas closed with the rousing refrain:

> Shout, shout, we're gaining ground,
> Hallelujah!
> We'll shout old Satan's kingdom down,
> Hallelujah![1]

The expression of those rugged pioneers may have lacked sophistication, but their note of confidence, that joyous assur-

---

[1] G. P. Jackson, *Down East Spirituals and Others* (New York: J. J. Augustine, 1939), pp. 232, 265.

ance of conquest of the enemy, sounds very much like the victors' shout around the throne in chapter 12.

Before moving on to describe the final destruction of the wicked, this interlude pictorially explains why the saints in this world face continual opposition. What the first-century church was going through at the hands of Caesar was but one immediate example of the much more pervasive and agelong conflict between the Lord of heaven and the powers of darkness. By perceiving the underlying reason for the warfare and its spiritual essence, the persecuted church can persevere in the strength of her victorious Lord.

The vision begins with a sign in heaven, of a pregnant woman, robed with the sun, like a resplendent bride clothed with light (12:1; cf., Psa. 104:2). Beneath her feet is the moon, symbolic of her dominion; upon her head rests a crown of twelve stars, representative of her royal estate. She symbolizes Israel, or the church (Gen. 37:9), the mother of God's people (Gal. 4:26; Isa. 54:1). About to give birth, the woman cries out in travail to be delivered (12:2; cf., Isa. 26:17; Isa. 66:7; Micah 4:10; Micah 5:3).

Standing before the woman, as a second sign, is a great red dragon, typifying the devil (12:3; cf., Isa. 27:1; Psa. 74:14; Ezk. 29:3; Job 40:18). He has seven heads and ten horns, descriptive of his complete rule (cf., Dan. 7:7,24). On his heads are crowns of arrogated authority, a power which he displays by hurling many stars to the earth (12:4; cf., Dan. 8:10). Showing his murderous enmity against God, the monster waits to devour the child as soon as the woman gives birth, a plan which we see enacted through human puppets during the birth and ensuing life of Jesus. The actors in this evil plot are depraved men, but the instigator of the conspiracy is "the devil and Satan, who deceives the whole world" (12:9).

The woman gives birth to a man-child, the promised Messiah, who is destined "to rule all the nations with a rod of iron" (12:5). Again the imagery relates to the Second Psalm, which speaks of God's Son breaking up the consolidated despotic powers of evil on the earth (Psa. 2:9). Like a Shepherd who protects His flock from wild beasts, He will smite those who have molested His people (cf., 19:15). This becomes apparent when Christ, conqueror over death and the grave, is "caught up to God" in the heavenly ascension and assumes His exalted reign on the throne (12:5).

Meanwhile, the messianic community, portrayed by the woman, flees into the wilderness, a place of spiritual consolation, where the church is nourished by God during the period of her great persecution (12:6; cf., 11:2; 13:5). The people of the covenant are often in circumstances which necessitate flight away from demonic afflictors, but in these difficult times God's tender care is unfailing (cf., Hos. 2:14; Ex. 16:4-36; 1 Kings 17:2,3; 1 Kings 19:3,4). Some readers interpret this scene as God's hiding place during a period of unprecedented tribulation.

Against this backdrop, a war is described in heaven. Satan seems to have attempted to acquire a place of rule at the throne of God, and he is challenged by Michael and his angels. In the ensuing struggle, the hosts of God are victorious, and the defeated dragon and his cohorts are cast down to earth (12:7-9). Perhaps this was alluded to by Jesus when He said, "I was watching Satan fall from heaven like lightning" (Luke 10:18). However the time sequence of God's conquest over Satan may be understood, the power of the pretender has been broken forever—Satan never again can rise to contest divine authority, though for a period, he has been permitted to exercise influence in the kingdoms of this world (Luke 4:6; John 12:31; John 14:30; John 16:11).[2]

It is this present dominion of Satan on planet earth which

---

[2] One may wonder why God did not immediately cast Satan into hell, knowing that he would beguile man to sin and thereby bring the human race under judgment. Though no answer can take away the mystery, still it can be observed that the demonic presence in this world now creates a

precipitates the trials of the church. Unable any longer to touch the Son, he has turned his anger upon the man-child's people—those "who keep the commandments of God and hold to the testimony of Jesus" (12:17). To be unmindful of his designs and the demons at his command, would be deadly. Our warfare is not against flesh and blood, but against satanic principalities, against rulers of darkness, against forces of evil in the spirit world (Eph. 6:12). By every insidious device of hell, the devil seeks to tear down the work of God. He is the instigator of sin and betrayal (Gen. 3:4,5; John 13:2). He tempts and slanders the righteous (John 1:9,10; Matt. 4:11). He inflicts suffering on the innocent (Job 2:7). He sows discord (Matt. 13:38,39); he removes the good seed of the Gospel (Matt. 13:19); he blinds the eyes of unbelievers (2 Cor. 4:4). He prowls about like a roaring lion, seeking whom he may devour (1 Peter 5:8). From the beginning of our days on this earth until the very end, we are engaged in a mortal conflict with the dragon.

### The Victorious Church

But the church is triumphant. Satan is a defeated foe. In the clear light of heaven, a shout is heard from the celestial hosts, so loud that it sounds like a single voice, saying: "Now the salvation, and the power, and the kingdom of our God and the authority of His Christ have come, for the accuser of our brethren has been thrown down, who accuses them before our God day and night" (12:10). The conquest of Satan guarantees that the Christian can live victoriously. It is a reality *now*. God has brought deliverance; His authority over

---

situation whereby man—through anguish, especially in a vicarious relationship—can learn ever greater depths of holy love. As the ultimate cause of all suffering, then, the devil actually fulfills a beneficial function in the divine economy.

the enemy is demonstrated and His reign established. The Anointed of God participates in this rule, because it was through His death and Resurrection that the power of Satan was brought to naught.

In consequence of this fact, the devil has no way by which he can condemn the brethren. The blameless One, whom Satan could never lay a charge against, by His sacrifice has taken away the guilt of mankind and thereby removed any grounds for an accusation to be made. Even more, the accuser no longer can even enter the courtroom to prefer a charge against the elect, for he has been disbarred from practice—cast out from the presence of the Judge (cf., Rom. 8:33,34).

Amanda Smith, a beloved black evangelist, used to tell about a confrontation with the devil on one of her journeys, when she was reminded of all her past sins.

"Now what do you say?" the accuser sneered.

Whereupon Amanda, without even bothering to look around, said, "Drive on, Gabriel, drive on!"

That is the response of the saved ones to the attack of the devil. We do not have to listen to his recriminations, for there is "now no condemnation for those who are in Christ Jesus" (Rom. 8:1). He has set us free.

It is not a mere passive freedom that the saints experience. As the next verse indicates, the church has an active role in the defeat of Satan. "They overcame him because of the blood of the Lamb and because of the word of their testimony, and they did not love their life even to death" (12:11).

The reference to the Lamb's blood, a recurring theme through the songs, stresses again the efficacy of the vicarious offering of Christ. Through the voluntary giving of Himself unto death, He has rendered "powerless him who had the power of death, that is, the devil" (Heb. 2:14; cf., 1 John 3:8). The shackles of sin have been broken; the grave has lost its prey.

Billy Graham tells of a time early in his ministry, when,

after preaching one night to a great crowd in the Cotton Bowl in Dallas, there was little response to his message. As he was leaving the platform, a dear old saint came up to him, put his arm around him, and said, "Billy, you didn't preach the cross tonight. Your message was good, but you didn't preach the cross." The great evangelist went to his room and wept. Then he made a resolve: "O God, so help me, there will never be a sermon that I preach unless the cross is central."[3]

Herein is the essence of the overcoming message. It is the blood—the all-conquering cross of God's eternal Son. By the blood of the Lamb, the church is victorious.

Believing the Gospel, commits one to proclaim it. Thus, built into the saving message is the principle of reproduction. One does not have to be a trained theologian or gifted preacher. One simply declares what he has seen and heard, not as a credal statement, but as a personal, living experience.

The relationship between the triumph of the church and the word of testimony may be seen in Peter's confession of Christ at Caesarea Philippi, after which Jesus said that upon this rock He would build His church, "and the gates of Hades shall not overpower it" (Matt. 16:18). What a masterful plan of conquest! When the Son of God is lifted up by His followers, hearers of the Word are called to believe on Him, and as they in turn tell others, the good news is destined to spread from person to person, until everyone has heard. Through this simple process of multiplication, nothing in this world can keep the church from storming the gates of hell.[4]

---

[3] Billy Graham, "Evangelism: Message and Method," *Christianity Today* III, no. 22 (August 3, 1959): 3.

[4] This promise is sometimes read in a defensive way, as if the church will not be overwhelmed by the assaults of hell. While this is true, a better interpretation of the verse sees the church on the attack, relentlessly pressing the claims of Christ until, at last, the powers of the underworld

What makes the testimony so undefeatable is the willingness of the witnesses to die for it: "they did not love their lives so much as to shrink from death" (12:11 NIV). Significantly, the word *witness* translates literally "martyr," and that is exactly what one becomes in following the Lamb. One cannot be His disciple without renouncing all self-rights, taking up the cross, and living in obedience to the will of God (Matt. 16:24). They that follow Christ have crucified the flesh, with its desires (Gal. 5:24), and reckon themselves dead to sin (Rom. 6:11).

Henri Nouwen tells of a Lutheran bishop who was imprisoned in a German concentration camp during World War II. An SS officer tried, through beating, to force a confession from him. Though the intensity of the torture increased, it could not break the bishop's silence. Finally, the infuriated officer, pounding his victim with even harder blows, shrieked, "But don't you know that I can kill you?" The bishop looked in the eyes of his torturer and said, "Yes, I know—do what you want—but I have already died."[5]

Instantly, as though paralyzed, the officer could no longer raise his arm. It was as if power over the bishop had been taken from him. All his cruelties had been based on the assumption that the bishop's physical life was his most precious possession and therefore he would be willing to make any concession to save it. But with the grounds for violence gone, torture was futile.

This was what the Roman world learned about the Christian martyrs. Nothing could beat them down—neither imprisonment, nor beatings, nor even the threat of death—

are overcome. For a discussion of this passage in its context, see my note in *The Mind of the Master* (Old Tappan: Fleming H. Revell Co., 1977), pp. 112, 113.

[5] Henri J. M. Nouwen, *Reaching Out: The Three Movements of Spiritual Life* (New York: Doubleday & Co., Inc., 1975), p. 84.

because they had died already with Christ. In losing their lives, they found life (Matt. 16:25). The power of the resurrection throbbed in their souls. Whether they lived or died made no difference, for they were the Lord's (Rom. 14:8).

## Living in Triumph

God's people are always to live with this inner victory. "For this reason," the voice continues, "rejoice, O heavens and you who dwell in them" (12:12). There is no place in heaven for a sad face or a troubled spirit.

But "Woe to the earth and the sea; because the devil has come down to you, having great wrath, knowing that he has only a short time" (12:12). We need to realize that in these closing days of history, the devil will use every weapon in his armory in an intensifying attack against the church. The increasing hostility does not indicate a strengthening of demonic power; rather, it is the last, desperate effort of an adversary who realizes that he is doomed.

As the attacks of the enemy mount, let us meet them with a sense of destiny, knowing that the days of conflict are coming to an end. Remember, too, that however fierce the battle, nothing "shall be able to separate us from the love of God, which is in Christ Jesus our Lord" (Rom. 8:39).

The secret is in the inner experience of the cross—that joyous dedication to fulfill the will of God, whatever the cost. Our understanding of the meaning of the cross deepens as we follow our Lord, to be sure, but at any time, we should be willing to respond to all that we know of His Word. In this daily abiding, we can know the triumph of Christ. When the inner battle is won, we can face confidently the battle raging in the world around us. For "in all these things we overwhelmingly conquer through Him who loved us" (Rom. 8:37).

In the third century, Cyprian, the bishop of Carthage,

wrote a letter to a friend, in which he set forth a timeless observation:

> If I could ascend some high mountain and look out over this wide land, you know very well what I would see. Robbers on the high roads, pirates on the seas, in the amphi-theaters men murdered to please applauding crowds, selfishness and cruelty, misery and despair under all roofs. It is a bad world—an incredibly bad world. But in the midst of it, I have found a quiet and a holy people who have learned a great secret. They are the despised and the persecuted, but they care not. They have overcome the world. These people are called Christians, and I am one of them.[6]

Such are Christian witnesses in every age. Though buffeted by many foes, they care not, for they have overcome the world. And in that confidence, the church goes forth with a song of victory.

> Crowns and thrones may perish,
>     Kingdoms rise and wane,
> But the Church of Jesus
>     Constant will remain;
> Gates of hell can never
>     'Gainst that Church prevail;
> We have Christ's own promise,
>     And that cannot fail.
>
> Onward, then, ye people,
>     Join our happy throng,
> Blend with ours your voices
>     In the triumph song;

---

[6] Quoted by Marvin J. Hartman in "Proclamation," *Vital Christianity*, November 5, 1967, p. 1.

Glory, laud, and honor
Unto Christ the King;
This through countless ages
Men and angels sing.

SABINE BARING-GOULD

# 12

# *The Song of Moses and the Lamb*

"Great and marvelous are Thy works, O Lord God, the
Almighty; Righteous and true are Thy ways, Thou King
of the nations. Who will not fear, O Lord, and glorify
Thy name? For Thou alone art holy; For all the nations
will come and worship before Thee, For Thy righteous
acts have been revealed."

REVELATION 15:3,4

## Victors Over the Beast

Aware that the mortally wounded devil, in the rage of defeat, will be more frantic in his attacks as the end approaches,
the victorious church learns of the appearance of two beasts
that reflect the satanic strategy (13:1–18; cf., Dan. 7:1–28).
The first rises out of the murky sea, a symbol of evil. Speaking
blasphemies against God and making war against His saints,
this predominant monster receives the homage of the world.
In his immediate form, the beast suggests the political and
military power of pagan Rome, while his broader influence
points to the deification of all worldly power. As a personal
manifestation, he has the form of the Antichrist (cf., 2 Thess.
2:4).

The second beast comes out of the earth, descriptive of a
state under satanic control. Speaking as a dragon in the guise
of a gentle lamb, he is a deceiver and false prophet, whose
chief aim is to make "the earth and those who dwell in it to
worship the first beast" (13:12). Through the performance of
miraculous deeds on the one hand and economic sanctions on

the other, he succeeds in bringing the greater part of mankind under his mark of 666.[1] All who do not pledge him allegiance face martyrdom.

After this terrible picture of the beast and his followers, a word of encouragement is in order, so the scene shifts to heaven, where the Lamb is seen standing upon a counterpart of Mount Zion (14:1). He is being praised by the redeemed, who have His mark in their foreheads, in contrast to those on earth who bear the mark of the beast. We are told that it is a "new song" (14:3) and has "the sound of many waters . . . like the sound of loud thunder and . . . like the sound of harpists playing on their harps" (14:2; cf., Ezk. 1:24; Ezk. 43:2). Yet the words of the song are not recorded, and no one can learn them, except the 144,000 who had been purchased from the earth (14:3).

Angels then appear in sequence, each with a proclamation to earthlings. The first is a summons to reverence God, the Creator, as the universal duty of all men (14:6,7). If this is a last call for civilization to repent, there is no indication that the message is believed. There follows a prophecy of the fall of the world's system of godliness, portrayed as "Babylon the great" (14:8; cf., 16:9; 17:5; 18:2,10,21; Dan. 4:30; Isa. 21:9; Jer. 51:7). It leads to a terrifying description of God's wrath awaiting all who have the mark of the beast (14:9–11; cf., Isa.

---

[1] It was common in apocalyptic literature to use numbers for letters of the alphabet and thereby produce a cryptogram of a word, readily decipherable by one who knew the formula. Doubtless the readers of this letter in the first century were in a better position to make this deduction than are persons now, which might explain the great diversity of interpretations, all the way from a contemporary Roman emperor to some modern demagogue of the twentieth century. In view of the situation, discretion should cause us to hold any identification tentative. But of this we can be reasonably sure: 6 is the number of incompleteness—that is, less than the perfect number 7—and hence comes to be associated with man. 666 as the trinity of 6 would speak of a being inferior to God, though illustrious and powerful. Some see in the number a symbol of the beast's repeated failure to attain his desired end.

51:17; Jer. 25:15-38; Job. 21:20; Psa. 75:8). Though faithfulness to Christ may bring death, those who die in the Lord shall enter into eternal blessedness (14:12,13).

John then sees the Son of Man, wearing the victor's golden wreath, coming to reap the harvest upon earth (14:14-16). This scene apparently refers to the calling forth of the redeemed, though not specified (cf., Matt. 13:30,39; Matt. 24:30,31). Still another figure depicts an angel thrusting in a sharp sickle, gathering the vintage of retribution, and casting it into the winepress of God's wrath (14:17-20). Just as Jesus suffered outside the gate (Heb. 13:12; John 19:20), so those who reject Him will be "trodden outside the city"; their blood flows as deep as the horses' bridles and reaches across the length of the land (14:20).[2] Then, in another sign, seven angels are seen in heaven, ready to pour out the seven last plagues upon the earth, which will complete God's wrath (15:1). But before the final scene is depicted, the praise service about the throne again captivates the viewer.

A great chorus of believers is seen standing by the sea of glass, previously likened to crystal (4:6), but here "mixed with fire," possibly alluding to the fiery persecutions through which they have come, as well as God's judgments (15:2). In their hands are "harps of God," accenting their song of praise (cf., Psa. 81:2). These are people who have "come off victorious from the beast and from his image and from the number of his name" (15:2), blessed ones, who would not bow the knee to the god of this world, or accept his apostate mark. They belong to that group mentioned earlier: those who have kept themselves pure from the allurements of sin and follow the Lamb in unquestioning obedience (14:4). In this devotion, they are unto God as the firstfruits of the harvest and an ear-

---

[2] Some interpreters treat both of these judgments as relating to the unrepentant. Others see them as describing the saints' impending martyrdom.

nest of the blessings to come. In contrast to the corrupt society of the world, they are pure: No lie has touched their lips, and lust has not defiled their minds (14:5; cf., Eph. 5:27; Phil. 2:15; Col. 1:22; Jude 24). Overcomers, indeed, of whom the world is not worthy.

## King of the Nations

They are singing of God's wonderful acts in the redemption of His people—"the song of Moses the bond-servant of God and the song of the Lamb" (15:3). The revelation of the old covenant combines with that of the new, and the law harmonizes with the Gospel, in another beautiful exclamation of praise.

The specific reference of Moses' hymn was to the mighty deliverance of the Israelites from bondage in Egypt. We can picture them there by the Red Sea, seeing the bodies of Pharaoh's soldiers washed upon the shore, as they sing:

The Lord is my strength and song,
And He has become my salvation;
This is my God, and I will praise Him. . . .
Pharaoh's chariots and his army He has cast into the sea . . .
The deeps cover them;
They went down into the depths like a stone.
Thy right hand, O Lord, is majestic in power,
Thy right hand, O Lord, shatters the enemy. . . .
Who is like Thee among the gods, O Lord?
Who is like Thee, majestic in holiness,
Awesome in praises, working wonders? . . .
In Thy lovingkindness Thou hast led the people whom Thou hast
    redeemed;
In Thy strength Thou hast guided them to Thy holy habitation. . . .
Thou wilt bring them and plant them in the mountain of . . . Thy
    dwelling,

The sanctuary, O Lord, which Thy hands have established.
The Lord shall reign forever and ever.

EXODUS 15:2,4–6,11,13,17,18

So memorable was this exodus that the song became a reg-
ular part of each Sabbath-evening's worship in Jewish synagogues. Its theme was etched in the heart of every child of
the covenant, foreshadowing a more wonderful salvation to
come. Just as God brought His people out of bondage in this
world, He will bring them into a promised land of eternal
rest. The leader of this greater exodus is the Lamb, who,
through the offering of His blood, has obtained for all who
believe, deliverance from sin and entrance into His kingdom.
The remembrance of it occasions this hymn to our mighty
Saviour.

"Great and marvelous are Thy works," they sing, "O Lord
God, the Almighty; righteous and true are Thy ways, Thou
King of the nations" (15:3).[3] Like the Psalms of old, the song
magnifies the incomparable excellence of Him who sits upon
the throne. "How great are Thy works, O Lord!" (Psa. 92:5;
cf., Psa. 111:2); "O sing to the Lord a new song, for He has
done wonderful things, His right hand and His holy arm have
gained the victory for Him" (Psa. 98:1; cf., Psa. 139:14); "The
Lord is righteous in all His ways, and kind in all His deeds"
(Psa. 145:17). It is the familiar exaltation of the attributes of
God, the Sovereign of the universe, the eternal King of the
nations.

In view of His greatness, a rhetorical question is asked:
"Who will not fear, O Lord, and glorify Thy name?" The

---

[3] The phrase "King of the ages" sometimes will be substituted for
"King of the nations" (e.g., the New International Version, New English
Bible, Revised Standard Version, Living Bible). Both have about equal
manuscript support. *Nations*, however, harmonizes more with the theme
of verse 4. The King James Version translates this title "King of saints."

grammatical form accents an obvious answer, which, in this case, is the most elemental duty of man. That it is the only reasonable conclusion is further explicated with the declaration, "For Thou alone art holy" (15:4). This theme, emphasized often around the throne, speaks of the total quality of God's perfection, entitling Him to perpetual worship. As His people had celebrated through the ages, "There is no one holy like the Lord, Indeed, there is no one besides Thee" (1 Sam. 2:2). So let them praise His "great and awesome name; Holy is He" (Psa. 99:3).

This adoration characterizes the messianic age, a fact affirmed in the next phrase, "for all the nations will come and worship before Thee" (15:4). The time has long been foreseen, when God's name "will be great among the nations," extending "from the rising of the sun, even to its setting" (Mal. 1:11). As the Psalmist said, "All nations whom Thou hast made shall come and worship before Thee, O Lord; And they shall glorify Thy name" (Psa. 86:9).

In the conclusion of the song, a final reason for magnifying the Lord is the administration of justice, for as the singers declare, "Thy righteous acts have been revealed" (15:4). God's absolute incompatibility with oppression and inhumanity is manifest to all. "He has revealed His righteousness in the sight of the nations. . . . All the ends of the earth have seen the salvation of our God" (Psa. 98:2,3).

It is interesting that in this lyric exaltation, not a word is said about the accomplishments of the overcoming Christians. Attention focuses entirely on the excellency of the King. As R. H. Charles observes, "in the perfect vision of God, self is wholly forgotten."[4] The glory of the Lord so overwhelms the saints that the difficulties over which they have triumphed seem as nothing.

---

[4] R. H. Charles, *The Revelation of St. John* II, International Critical Commentary (Edinburgh: T & T Clark, 1920), p. 35.

## Transparent Worship

Such unassuming adoration is but natural, in the presence
of the King. And though spontaneous in heaven, it will rise
wherever He reigns in the hearts of His witnesses.

A story that comes out of the early church is a stirring example.[5] In the year A.D. 320, in a vain effort to impede the
growth of the church, the Roman Emperor Valerius Licinius
decreed that all civil servants and members of the military
must offer sacrifice before the local gods. One cold, winter
morning, the order was read to the Twelfth Legion, stationed
at Sabaste in Armenia, and the soldiers were called upon to
demonstrate their loyalty to Caesar through the prescribed
offering. But there were forty Christians in the ranks of the
legion, who informed their captain that they could not sacrifice on a pagan altar.

The commander was dismayed. Dare these men defy the
emperor? Yet, knowing they had proven their bravery many
times on the field of battle and not wanting to inflict punishment upon them, he ordered the Christian soldiers placed in
confinement overnight, to reconsider their decision. Next
morning they were brought forth and again commanded to
worship the pagan gods. Again they refused. "We have made
our choice," they said. "We shall devote our love to our
God."

At this, the captain grew angry and ordered the men

---

[5] It appears in the nineteenth homily of Basil of Caesarea, and an account is also in the writings of Gregory of Nyssa. A more recent narrative, edited by Oscar van Gebhardt, was published by Alexander
Duncher in Berlin, 1902. Achilles Arroamides translated this for *Decision* magazine, edited by Sherwood E. Wirt, © December 1963 by the
Billy Graham Evangelistic Association, pp. 8, 9, from which this abbre-
viated account is taken and used with permission of the Billy Graham
Evangelistic Association. Doubtless some legendary elements have found
their way into the story, though there is no doubt about the historical
substance of the death of the forty martyrs during the persecution of
Licinius.

bound over in custody of the jailer, to await arrival of the general who would pass sentence. During this period of imprisonment, often the soldiers could be heard singing psalms of praise to their God. When the general arrived, the men were informed that if they did not obey the emperor's decree, they would be delivered over for torture. Unshaken, the Christians replied: "You can have our armor, and our bodies as well. We prefer Christ!"

Early the following morning, sentence was pronounced. The men were to be led to the shore of a nearby frozen lake, and there, at sundown, they were to be stripped and escorted out to the middle of the ice, to await death by freezing. Because of their high reputation for valor, however, the general had ordered that they be given the privilege of recanting at any time. To encourage this, a heated bathhouse on the shore was readied for any of the soldiers who were willing to renounce their faith and return to the comfort of the world.

A bitter wind whipped over the lake's surface as the men were driven out, shivering in the dusk. Guards were posted on the shore, among them the jailer in whose custody they had been kept during their days of imprisonment.

Then one of the forty soldiers lifted his voice out on the lake and began to sing. He was soon joined by the others:

> Forty soldiers for Christ!
> We shall not depart from You as long as You give us life.
> We shall call upon Your name whom all creation praises.
> On You we have hoped, and we are not ashamed.

Lustily they sang, while the ice chilled their feet. The night air resounded with one song of praise after another. But as the hours passed, their songs grew more feeble, until finally they could not be heard by the men on shore.

Then a strange thing happened. One of the forty was seen emerging from the darkness, staggering toward the shore. The guards posted there were dozing, except the jailer, who

through the night stood motionless, peering out upon the
lake, his ears straining to catch the mumbled prayers of the
dying Christians.

"Thirty-nine good soldiers of Christ," came a thin, fal-
tering voice from the distance. The jailer watched the man
fall to his knees and crawl into the bathhouse.

At that moment, something happened in the heart of the
jailer. Only he and God will ever know what it was. But the
guards reported hearing a shout that woke them from their
sleep. Opening their eyes, they saw the jailer wrench off his
armor and run to the lake. Lifting his right hand, he cried,
"There are forty good soldiers of Christ!" Then, marching
out on the ice into the darkness, he began to sing:

> We shall not depart from You as long as You give us life.
> We shall call upon Your name whom all creation praises.
> On You we have hoped, and we were not ashamed.

In the morning the forty men, including the jailer, were
found in the middle of the lake, huddled together in a frozen
heap. As the captain watched their bodies being carted away,
suddenly he turned to one of the guards and demanded,
pointing to the jailer, "What is he doing there?"

"We cannot understand it, captain," replied a guard. "It
was far into the night, when all of a sudden he jumped to his
feet, shouted something, stripped off his armor, and ran out
on the lake."

"Was he bewitched?" the captain asked.

"Probably, sir. Ever since those Christians came under his
care, we have noticed something different about him. At
times he would be singing under his breath. It was a bad sign,
we decided. Too much music is bad for soldiers. Makes them
strange. Don't you think so, captain?"

Yes, too much singing in the Spirit does seem odd, in a
world that has no lasting joy. Such happy troubadours of song
are earth's misfits, but they are no strangers in heaven. And
one cannot be around them long, before sensing a tug, some-

thing of that pull of another world, where joy unceasingly erupts from love, and praise to the Lamb never ends.

> Come, thou almighty King,
> Help us thy name to sing,
>     Help us to praise!
> Father all glorious,
> O'er all victorious,
> Come, and reign over us,
>     Ancient of Days!
>
> To Thee, great One in Three,
> Eternal praises be,
>     Hence, evermore:
> Thy sovereign majesty
> May we in glory see,
> And to eternity
>     Love and adore!

ANONYMOUS

# 13

# *The Hallelujah Chorus*

"Hallelujah! Salvation and glory and power belong to
our God; Because His judgments are true and righteous;
for He has judged the great harlot who was corrupting
the earth with her immorality, and He has avenged the
blood of His bond-servants on her.... Hallelujah! Her
smoke rises up forever and ever... Amen. Hallelujah!"

REVELATION 19:1–4

## The Shouting Host

As the strains of the harpers and the song of the triumphant martyrs die away, John looks and sees that "the
temple of the tabernacle of the testimony in heaven was
opened," from which the seven angels emerge. One of the
living creatures about the throne hands them each a golden
bowl "full of the wrath of God," which may reiterate a relationship between the prayers of the saints and the final consummation of history (15:5–7; cf., 5:8). That plagues would
be associated with wrath recalls the judgments upon the
Egyptians, as well as God's covenant in Leviticus, "If then,
you act with hostility against Me and are unwilling to obey
Me, I will increase the plague on you seven times according
to your sins" (Lev. 26:21). The severity of these plagues has
led many interpreters to connect them with the third woe,
mentioned earlier (11:14). So awesome is the wrath of God
about to be poured out that "the temple was filled with
smoke from the glory of God and from His power; and no one

was able to enter the temple until the seven plagues of the seven angels were finished" (15:8).

There follows in rapid sequence the visitation of the plagues. The first is emptied upon the earth, and grievous sores came upon those who had the mark of the beast (16:1, 2). The second bowl is poured out upon the sea, and "it became blood like that of a dead man; and every living thing in the sea died" (16:3). The third bowl is dispersed upon the rivers and springs, with the same effect (16:4). At this point, the plagues become so nauseating that another voice speaks from heaven, to reassure that nothing is out of character with divine justice (16:5–7).

When the fourth bowl is poured out upon the sun, men are scorched with intense heat, but they still refuse to repent and glorify God (16:8,9). The fifth bowl is discharged upon the realm of the beast, darkening his domains, and men gnaw their tongues because of their pains and sores, though they remain unrepentant (16:10,11). As the contents of the sixth bowl are released upon the river Euphrates, its waters are dried up, enabling the kings of the east to invade the west, in preparation for the last battle of Armageddon (16:12–16). Finally, the seventh bowl is poured out upon the air, and the cities of the world crumble; Babylon the great is made to drink the cup of the wine of the fierceness of God's wrath. The earth quakes. Every island and mountain vanishes. Hailstones of a hundred-pound weight fall from the sky. The end has come (16:17–21). Yet the people remain hard and bitter, finally cursing God (16:21).[1]

Describing Babylon in more detail, John recapitulates the whole gauntlet of human rebellion (17:1–18:24). The city is

---

[1] This would remind us that these fearful plagues come upon persons who refuse to repent, indicating that there is the opportunity of turning to God, if there is a desire. The persistent refusal of the people to responsibly face the consequences of their sins is a sobering insight into the accumulative result of selfishness.

pictured as a great harlot, the mother of all the abominations of the world. Bedecked with gold and precious stones, she offers a cup, full of moral corruption, to anyone who will partake. Those who dwell on the earth become intoxicated with the wine of her seductive culture and commit fornication by worshiping at her idolatrous shrines. Drunk with the blood of the saints and martyrs, the pagan world system that she symbolizes, supported by the beastly powers of the Antichrist, makes war against the Lamb and His church. But, as stressed in other ways before, the confederation of evil is defeated by the "Lord of lords and King of kings" and His followers (17:14). Before the scene is over, the scarlet woman is ravaged by her own accomplices and left desolate, naked, and burning with fire. As the smoke of her destruction goes up, the kings of the earth, the merchants and seafarers who have trafficked in her pleasures, are so horrified at what they see that they stand afar off, repeating the dirge, "Woe, woe, the great city has fallen!"

But the account does not close with the lamentation of the world. "After these things," John hears the sound of jubilant singing in heaven (19:1). For the church, there is always the joy of the eternal morning after the sorrows of this earth's night. I remember a dear friend using this verse once in speaking at a memorial service for his wife. He reflected upon some of the suffering they had passed through during her last illness, as they watched helplessly while cancer pursued its relentless course. Yet with beautiful serenity in his voice, he said there had come the blessedness of God "after these things." After the long deathwatches are over, after the cruel conflicts have ceased, after the last attack of the evil one has taken its deadly toll, deliverance comes.

The hymn is lifted by "a great multitude in heaven," comprising the church triumphant (19:1). Earlier, the saints, apostles, and prophets had been called upon to rejoice because God had judged the harlot on their behalf (18:20), and now their praises peal forth in mighty strains of song. What a contrast to the mournful wails of the world's leaders, beholding the fall of Babylon.

## Praise to Jehovah

The shouting multitude begins its exaltation with a resounding "Hallelujah" (19:1). It comes from two Hebrew words which mean "praise" and "Jehovah." From early days, the word became a form of public exclamation, combining "the notions of admiration, adulation, and rejoicing."[2] The translation "Praise the Lord" occurs frequently in the Psalms, as a response to the works of God (Psalms 106; 111; 112; 113; 117; 135; 146–150), though only in this chapter in Revelation does the word appear in the New Testament.

Further accenting the expression of praise, the masses exclaim, "Salvation and glory and power belong to our God" (19:1).[3] Martin Franzmann observes: "The salvation He has wrought; the glory He has manifested; the power He has evinced."[4] These attributes recurring in the songs invoke in the heart of man an attitude of "gratitude, reverence, and trust."[5] Added to this are the qualities of truth and justice in the divine nature, "because His judgments are true and righteous; for He has judged the great harlot who was corrupting the earth with her immorality, and He has avenged the blood of His bond-servants on her" (19:2).

The statement sounds much like that of an angel, as the vials were emptied on the earth, "Righteous art Thou, who

---

[2] Colin Brown, ed., *The New International Dictionary of New Testament Theology* I (Grand Rapids: Zondervan, 1977), p. 99.

[3] The additional attribute of honor is found in some authorities, as noted in the King James Version.

[4] Martin H. Franzmann, *The Revelation to John* (St. Louis: Concordia, 1976), p. 125.

[5] William Barclay, *The Revelation of John* I, rev. ed. (Philadelphia: Westminster Press, 1976), p. 169.

art and who wast, O Holy One, because Thou didst judge
these things; for they poured out the blood of saints and
prophets, and Thou has given them blood to drink. They de-
serve it" (16:5,6). A free rendering of the last phrase might
read, "They got what was coming to them" (cf., Isa. 49:26).
Corroborating this sense of fairness, a voice, probably representing the martyrs (6:9) and the prayers of the saints (8:3-5),
comes from the altar, "Yes, O Lord God, the Almighty, true
and righteous are Thy judgments" (16:7).[6]

Judgments upon the rebellious earth invariably are associated in the songs with God's moral perfection. It is not
angry revenge, but righteous rectitude, which is celebrated.
Justice and truth have prevailed. Those who have disre-
garded God's law have been brought to utter ruin and shame.
The harlot and her devotees can no longer maim and kill the
beloved of God; the universe is rid of the seduction of sin.
And, in the demolition of evil, God confers upon His servants
a measure of His own honor.

The thought of its wonder is such that again the enraptured multitude exclaims, "Hallelujah!" Babylon's destruction is complete; "her smoke rises up forever and ever" (19:3;
cf., 14:11; 18:9,18). The expression recalls Isaiah's prophecy
against wicked Edom: "its land shall become burning pitch.
It shall not be quenched night or day; Its smoke shall go up
forever" (Isa. 34:9,10). It is a way of saying that the diabolical
world system is finished—gone forever. The smoke of the
burning rises to heaven, as a perpetual remembrance of
God's faithfulness to His Word.

The elders and the living creatures, always sensitive to the
reputation of God, join the heavenly shout. Falling down and
worshiping Him who sits on the throne, they say, "Amen.

---

[6] Actually, this message from the angel and the altar constitutes another song, as the term is used in this study, but since the content is not
appreciably different from others, it is not treated separately (cf., 6:10;
11:18; 15:4; 19:1,2).

Hallelujah!" (19:4) In brief ejaculations of praise, they affirm their agreement with all that has been voiced by the multitude, while also getting in their own declaration of praise to Jehovah. What more need be said? In the presence of such infinite majesty, more appropriate words would be hard to find.

### Everyone Join the Chorus

With this, a voice comes from the throne, calling upon all God's people to adore Him, a message that reaches down to the earth across the ages. "Give praise to our God, all you His bond-servants, you who fear Him, the small and the great" (19:5). Perhaps an angel, seeing the oppressed church still on earth, wanted to help us get our priorities in order. For, whatever our rank or station, however far along we may be in the pilgrimage of faith, the worship of God should be our highest joy. So, to use the words of Isaac Watts:

> Come, ye that love the Lord,
>     And let your joys be known:
> Join in a song with sweet accord,
>     While ye surround the throne.
>
> Let those refuse to sing
>     Who never knew our God;
> But children of the heavenly King
>     May speak their joys abroad.

That is why God has made us. We are His to praise Him— to adore Him—to fall down before Him—to worship Him forever. As the Psalmist sang, we are gathered "from among the nations, To give thanks to Thy holy name, And glory in Thy praise." Therefore, "From everlasting to everlasting . . . let all the people say, 'Amen.' Praise the Lord!" (Psa. 106:47, 48). The creature is never so invigorated as when engaged in this occupation.

In 1741, a minor poet, Charles Jenners, wrote a libretto

entitled "A Sacred Oratorio." The collection of biblical excerpts was sent to George Frederick Handel, with the reminder that "the Lord gave the Word."

The package came at a time when Handel was going through a severe depression. He had been rebuffed by England's nobility, business misfortunes had left him deeply in debt, and at fifty-seven years of age, tired of working, he had retreated into seclusion.

As the listless Handel leafed through the manuscript, his eyes fell upon the words: "He was despised and rejected of men . . . He looked for someone to have pity on Him, but there was no man; neither found He any to comfort Him."

With a growing feeling of identity, Handel read on: "He trusted in God . . . God did not leave His soul in hell . . . He will give you rest." The words began to throb within his breast. "Wonderful, Counselor, Mighty God, the Everlasting Father, Prince of Peace . . . I know that my Redeemer liveth . . . Rejoice . . . Hallelujah!"

Feeling the triumph of the heavenly song, Handel grabbed a pen and started writing. Music for the words began to flow through his mind with such swiftness that he could scarcely write the notes fast enough. For twenty-four days, the composer remained in his room on Hanover Street in London. His manservant would bring food to him, but often it was untouched. Sometimes he would take a piece of bread, start to eat, then let it drop from his hand, as some new inspiration called forth expression. His servant watched in astonishment as his master's tears dropped on the page and mingled with the ink. At times he would jump up and run to the harpsichord, waving his arms in the air, singing aloud, "Hallelujah! Hallelujah! Hallelujah!" Later Handel confided, "I think I did see all heaven before me, and the great God Himself."[7]

---

[7] For more details, see the accounts of the writing of the *Messiah* in Newman Flower, *George Frederic Handel* (New York: Charles Scribner's Sons, 1948), pp. 286–302; Robert Manson Myers, *Handel's Messiah* (New

Of a truth, he was caught up in another world. Never before had he experienced such religious exhilaration, nor would he ever know the same intensity of feeling again. But in those few days, when his mind was absorbed in the wonder and praise of God, this rather ordinary man gave to the world a musical composition that still lifts the soul heavenward whenever it is sung.

In one early performance of the cantata in London, as the "Hallelujah Chorus" was being sung, the king was so moved that he rose to his feet. The audience followed his example and remained standing until the end—a practice that has continued to this day.

It should not be surprising that the composition and rendition of *The Messiah* should lift people to nobler thoughts and actions. There is something elevating about the praise of God. When we magnify His name and celebrate His glory, our own souls partake of greatness. Imagine, then, what it will be like to hear the celestial choirs about the throne: even better, to be a part of that number.

Listen! They are singing now. Don't you hear them? The choirs of heaven are singing and shouting the praise of God. All creation is in celebration. "And He shall reign forever and ever, King of kings and Lord of lords, King of kings and Lord of lords, Hallelujah! Hallelujah! Hallelujah!"

> Praise, my soul, the King of heaven,
> To His feet thy tribute bring;
> Ransomed, healed, restored, forgiven,
> Evermore His praises sing.
> Allelujah! Allelujah!
> Praise the everlasting King!

---

York: Octagon Books, 1971), pp. 52–87; and the article by Doron K. Antrim, "The Miracle of the Messiah," *Christian Herald* (April 1948), pp. 25, 26.

Angels in the height, adore Him,
  Ye behold Him face to face;
Sun and moon, bow down before Him,
  Dwellers all in time and space.
Allelujah! Allelujah!
Praise with us the God of grace.

HENRY F. LYLE

# 14

# The Symphony of the Marriage Feast

"Hallelujah! For the Lord our God, the Almighty, reigns. Let us rejoice and be glad and give the glory to Him, for the marriage of the Lamb has come and His bride has made herself ready."

REVELATION 19:6,7

## The Voluminous Sound

It was said of George Whitefield that when he preached, his voice could be heard for a mile, but that when he sang, he could be heard for two miles.[1] Singing just carries farther.

I am not sure why this is true of the physical voice, but I can see a beautiful analogy with the spiritual songs of heaven. The worship of God brings vibrations of accord from all the universe, making the music more resonant as the works of creation catch up the melodious strains. Earth's discord is gone; nothing can encumber the harmony of praise. And as the number of voices multiplies, the symphonic sound of the whole becomes greater than its parts.

Here it is well to note that all the songs about the throne involve corporate worship. There are no solos. Yet such is the unity of spirit, that the myriads of participants sound as if

---

[1] Halford E. Luccock, *The Story of Methodism* (New York: Abingdon-Cokesbury, 1926), p. 105.

141

they have one voice. We should not miss the force of this truth upon our own lives. There is a discipline of worship that comes from joining with others of like precious faith. The uniqueness of each person has to be tuned to the master key and the causes of dissonance eliminated. Though harmony in song becomes more difficult as the number of singers increases, the resultant sound grows more beautiful and intense.

Imagine the majestic crescendo of heaven's "great multitude" (19:1; cf., 5:12; 12:1,10; 19:1), unrestrained by any selfish inhibitions, united as a single voice of praise (19:6; cf., 5:12; 12:10; 19:1). This is the sound John heard, as all the hosts about the throne—the seraphim and cherubim; the white-robed elders; the angels and archangels; the blood-washed multitude that no man can number, from every tongue, tribe, people, and nation—all join in exaltation of their reigning King, soon to receive His espoused bride. The joyous shouting is likened to "the sound of many waters," as though a thousand Niagaras were cataracting over steep cliffs, or a hundred oceans were crashing on the shore. To use another figure, it is compared to "the sound of mighty peals of thunder" (19:6), splitting the heavens in rolling sonic booms. Such dramatic language not only accentuates the voluminous joy of the multitude, but also prepares us to recognize the power and glory of the One addressed (cf., 1:15; 14:2; Ezk. 1:24; Ezek. 43:2; Dan. 10:6).

## The Bridegroom Comes

"Hallelujah," they cry, "For the Lord our God, the Almighty, reigns" (19:6). This is another acclamation of the omnipotence of God, sovereign over heaven and earth, who holds in His hand the scepter of eternal righteousness. He, not Caesar, rules in undisputed control. Yet, wonder of wonders, this great Potentate, the King of glory, the Lord God Almighty, is "our God"—He is personally related to His people, so that we are His and He is ours.[2]

Enraptured with the contemplation of their blessing, members of the heavenly throng exhort themselves: "Let us rejoice and be glad and give the glory to Him" (19:7). It is interesting that Jesus uses this same combination of verbs when He says to the persecuted, "Rejoice, and be glad, for your reward in heaven is great" (Matt. 5:12). Whether or not the throne hosts have in mind their Lord's words, they are certainly knowledgeable that His promise has come true.

"For," as they declare, "the marriage of the Lamb has come and His bride has made herself ready" (19:7). At last the sacrificial Lamb of God will gather His church to Himself in eternal wedlock. The bond of marriage, as a symbol of the relationship between God and His beloved, occurs again and again in Scripture. Isaiah spoke of Israel's "Maker" as the "husband" and the people as "a wife of one's youth" (Isa. 54:5,6). Hosea depicted the Lord telling the children of the covenant, "I will betroth you to Me forever" (Hos. 2:19; cf., Hos. 2:20). Even in its backslidden state, Israel was married to God, according to Jeremiah (Jer. 3:14). In the Gospels, Jesus likens the kingdom of heaven to a king who made a marriage feast for his son and sent forth his servants, to call those who were bidden to the wedding (Matt. 22:1–10; cf., Matt. 25:1; Mark 2:19). Then, too, there is Paul's comparison of Christ's love for His church with a husband's love for his wife (Eph. 5:25–32).

In biblical times, the betrothal of a bride was an event separate from the wedding. Though the engaged couple were

---

[2] Some authorities leave out the "our" in this phrase, perhaps because in the other passages where "the Lord God, the Almighty" occurs, the possessive pronoun is not found (1:8; 4:8; 11:17; 15:3; 16:7; 21:22). However, the word does appear in many of the better manuscripts, and although it brings a new dimension to the divine title, there is no compelling reason why it should be excluded.

considered as husband and wife and remained loyal to each
other, they lived apart until the actual consummation of the
marriage on the wedding day.[3] On that day, the wedding
party assembled at the house of the groom, where he, accompanied by his groomsmen and friends, proceeded to the house
of the bride. There the bride and her attendant maidens and
friends joined the party and were escorted to the house of the
groom. As they moved through the streets, everyone rose to
salute the procession, and it was deemed almost a religious
duty to speak of the bride's beauty and virtue. Arriving at the
house, they completed the formal ceremony, after which, everyone joined in a great wedding feast. It was a festive occasion, with dancing and singing and great merriment.[4]

When Christ's marriage with His church is seen in this
context, we can understand how, by faith, persons can already be joined to Him in betrothal, though the union is not
finalized until He comes as the Bridegroom, to meet His
bride and take her back with Him to the Father's house for
the marriage supper. The church lives now in faithfulness to
her espoused husband; we wait for the glorious appearing of
our Lord with His heavenly host, to receive us to Himself and
escort us home, to dwell with Him forever.

In the ensuing narrative, the Bridegroom's coming is described. Christ is seen riding upon a white horse, accompanied by the armies of heaven, bringing destruction upon the

[3] This period of engagement could last up to twelve months, during
which time the parties, except for living together, were considered married. Any breach of this contract would be treated as adultery, and the
relationship could not be dissolved without formal divorce, just as with
marriage. A good discussion of the custom is in Alfred Edersheim, *The
Life and Times of Jesus the Messiah* I (Grand Rapids: Wm. B. Eerdmans,
1972), pp. 148–150; 352–354. Incidentally, this practice explains why
Joseph would be called the husband of Mary during their engagement
"before they came together" in marriage (Matt. 1:18–20).
[4] *Ibid.* I, pp. 354, 355; *ibid.* II, p. 455.

enemies of God (19:11–21). The subsequent account of the period of blessedness on earth (20:1–6) and the unloosing of Satan for a season (20:7–10), climaxing in the final judgment at the great, white throne (20:11–15), adds more detail. Though the picture may be variously interpreted, especially in chronology, it seems that the marriage supper refers to a time following the completion of the other events related to the Second Coming of Christ.

What is most significant for us is that when the King comes, His bride is properly attired to meet Him. "It was given to her to clothe herself in fine linen, bright and clean; for the fine linen is the righteous acts of the saints" (19:8).[5] The focus is upon practical holiness: a life of loving obedience to the Word of God. Nothing here is theoretical. This is the kind of piety that we read about in the Acts of the Apostles, a positive virtue that finds expression in deeds of mercy and truth. Lest we imagine that such works flow from human initiatives, the revelator takes care to point out that this righteous covering for the wedding feast is "given" by the Lamb—it is a tribute to the grace of God.

How fitting that the songs of heaven should close on this note. They began with the recognition of a God thrice holy in His nature; now they conclude with the display of His holiness in the righteous acts of His church. From beginning to end, heaven's watchword is holiness unto the Lord.

---

[5] In an earlier description of the 144,000, they are compared to virgins "who have not been defiled with women" (14:4), a reference to their purity of devotion as Christ's promised bride. The true Israel is often seen in Scripture as a virgin (Jer. 18:13; Amos 5:2; 2 Kings 19:21), while the unfaithful are compared to a harlot (Jer. 3:6; Hos. 5:2). Anticipating their marriage, the followers of the Lamb have kept themselves unspotted from the world, in order that they might be presented to their Lord as a pure virgin (2 Cor. 11:2). In this, they have not played the harlot, as have the kings of the earth (17:2).

## Living in Readiness

"Blessed are those who are invited to the marriage supper of the Lamb" (19:9). The church is seen, in this beatitude, as both the bride and the guests invited to the wedding. Virtually the same blessing is heard on the lips of Jesus, when He says, "Blessed is everyone who shall eat bread in the kingdom of God" (Luke 14:15). Again He says that God's elect "will come from east and west, and from north and south, and will recline at table in the kingdom of God" (Luke 13:29). When taking the cup at the Last Supper, He told His disciples that henceforth, He would not drink of the fruit of the vine, until that day when He would drink it new with them, in the Father's kingdom (Matt. 26:29). The vision centers upon the marriage banquet in the new Jerusalem, when the messianic promises are fulfilled and the kingdom has come to fruition.[6]

Such are the true sayings of God, and all who heed them are blessed indeed. But one must "hold the testimony of Jesus" (19:10). This may be interpreted as the Lord's testimony to us or our witness of His Gospel in the world. Perhaps both meanings are intended. Herein is the essence of the prophetic Word.

For our part, we should be getting ready to meet the Bridegroom, when He comes. Where His Spirit shows our garments to be soiled by uncleanness, we must "cleanse ourselves from all defilement of flesh and spirit, perfecting holiness in the fear of God" (2 Cor. 7:1). Thanks to His grace, when there is honest confession of the sin, "He is faithful and righteous to forgive us our sins and to cleanse us from all unrighteousness" (1 John 1:9). Christ intends for His people to be holy. To this end, He gave Himself for us, "that He might

---

[6] It is worthy of mention that Jesus' first miracle was to gladden a wedding feast at Cana (John 2:1-11). However, on that occasion, He said that His hour was not yet come, a reference not only to Calvary, but to the ultimate marriage supper in the kingdom.

present to Himself the church in all her glory, having no spot or wrinkle or any such thing; but that she should be holy and blameless" (Eph. 5:27).

I remember well my own wedding day. It was June 3, 1951. As the time drew near, my bride, with one of her seamstress friends, began to make her wedding gown. Though we were observing the custom of the fiancé not seeing the bride in her dress until the wedding day, I was told something of its design and material and was sure that it was going to be the most beautiful dress that had ever been made.

At last the day came. I was standing at the altar of the church when the door opened and I saw for the first time my bride, coming down the aisle adorned in her wedding garment. Indeed, it was the most beautiful dress I had ever seen—a long, flowing, glistening, white satin gown, without any spot or wrinkle or any such thing. And as I looked into my beloved's face, I saw a love that corresponded to her wedding garment—a love that was pure, a love that reached out and embraced me with all that she was and hoped to be. The vows we took at the altar, pledging ourselves each to the other, were but a public affirmation of a love that was complete.

I have to say that in these intervening years, I have learned a great deal more about the meaning of those vows. There have been some strains, times of sorrow and suffering, but we have gone through them together, and the experiences through which we have passed have only made us more conscious of our love. Yet because our capacity to understand and appreciate each other has grown, it might be said that we love now more than we did then, even though in the beginning, as we knew in our hearts, we loved with all our souls, with all our minds, and with all our strength.

I have often thought that this is an illustration of the way Jesus wants us to love Him. However limited our comprehension of His will, He wants us to give all that we know of ourselves to all that we know of Him—to love and trust Him

with all that we are, all that we hope to be. This is the fulfillment of the law and the prophets (Matt. 22:37–40). It is the
bond of perfectness (Col. 3:14). In this devotion, we are to
live in exciting readiness, to meet Him when the shout is
heard, "Behold, the Bridegroom comes!"

> Let every act of worship be
> Like our espousals, Lord, to Thee:
> Like the blest hour, when from above
> We first received the pledge of love.
>
> The gladness of that happy day,
> O may it ever stay:
> Nor let our faith forsake its hold,
> Nor hope decline, nor love grow cold.
>
> Let every moment, as it flies,
> Increase Thy praise, improve our joys,
> Till we are raised to sing Thy name,
> At the great supper of the Lord.

ISAAC WATTS

# Epilogue: The City of Unceasing Song

God of my life, through all my days
My grateful powers shall sound Thy praise;
My song shall wake with opening light,
And cheer the dark and silent night.

When anxious cares would break my rest,
And griefs would tear my throbbing breast,
Thy tuneful praises, raised on high,
Shall check the murmur and the sigh.

But, O when that last conflict's o'er,
And I am chain'd to earth no more,
With what glad accents shall I rise
To join the music of the skies!

PHILIP DODDRIDGE

## The New Jerusalem

Heaven has been called by Christina Rossetti "the home-land of music." It is a fitting description, for as we have observed in this study of communication about the throne, the praise of the King is the only language that has any relevance, where Christ is Lord of all. Whatever is not reflective of this reality would be totally out of place in His kingdom of perfect love. Joyous song simply accents the harmonic union of creation with the glory of God.

The sound of singing increased, John Bunyan writes in *The*

*Pilgrim's Progress,* as Christian and Hopeful entered the land
of Beulah, beyond the Valley of the Shadow of Death. When
their eyes finally beheld the city of God, such was its beauty
that they fell sick with happiness, crying out because of their
pangs, "If you see my Beloved, tell Him I am sick with love."
So glorious was the city, reflected in the brilliant sunlight of
the cloudless day, that they could not as yet with open face
look upon it, but had to use an instrument made for the
purpose.[1]

John the apostle probably has something of this same feeling, as the vision of the church, now married to the Lamb,
comes to its conclusion. He sees "a new heaven and a new
earth; for the first heaven and the first earth passed away, and
there is no longer any sea" (21:1; cf., Isa. 65:17; Mark 13:31;
Rom. 8:19; 2 Peter 3:12). It is not the annihilation of the old
cosmos, but its transfiguration—resolving the universe into
its basic substance, splitting its atoms, freeing its elements
from all restrictions, and then making out of it a new order of
creation. The change might be compared to a piece of coal
placed in a retort, and through the application of extreme
heat, made fluid as gas, after which it crystallizes into a transparent diamond. By "making all things new" (21:5), God simply brings His creation to a higher form of materiality—
matter ruled by the Spirit. True, because of our earthly
bondage now, it is impossible to speak of this new order, except in pictures and parables, but this does not imply mere
allegory: Heaven is an actual, existing, spiritual reality.[2]

---

[1] John Bunyan, *The Pilgrim's Progress* (New York: Peter Pauper Press),
pp. 148, 149. Every Christian can find himself in this allegory, which I
believe is one of the greatest compositions ever written, outside of
Scripture.

[2] Though the pictures help us to imagine the incomprehensible reality, the reality itself is more beautiful than we can imagine. In contrast,
that which is evil always appears more attractive in imagination.

Into this glorified atmosphere appears "the holy city, new Jerusalem, coming down out of heaven from God, made ready as a bride adorned for her husband" (21:2).[3] As already noted, the divine nature of holiness characterizes the habitation of God's elect. No one who is unclean can enter this home of the saints (21:8; 22:15). That it is called a city, a community of shared dependence and responsibility, again reflects the corporate nature of the church. Prefigured by the holy city of David, "where great is the Lord, and greatly to be praised" (Psa. 48:1), the new Jerusalem will never be marred by deceit or disrupted by disunity.

### God With Us

The seer's gaze is still fixed on the city when he hears someone speaking out of the throne. "Behold, the tabernacle of God is among men, and He shall dwell among them, and they shall be His people" (21:3). The announcement recalls the promise made through Moses: "I will make My dwelling among you, and My soul will not reject you. I will also walk among you and be your God, and you shall be My people"

---

[3] As inferred earlier, the appearance of the new Jerusalem may follow a reign of blessedness of the church on earth, or it may come immediately after the marriage supper, depending upon how the millennium reign is interpreted (20:1–10). If one holds to a premillennial position, after Christ's return, He will reign on the earth with His people for 1000 years, after which will come a loosing of Satan for a season, followed by his final defeat and judgment, and then the state of the new creation. If an amillennial view prevails, the millennial description is spiritualized, to mean the church age following Christ's first advent, so that the new Jerusalem would come immediately after the presentation of the church in holy wedlock. The same idea would pertain in the case of a postmillennial outlook, although here it is believed that an age of blessedness will come on earth before Christ returns. Regardless of the way the millennium may be understood, however, the new Jerusalem represents the eternal state of the kingdom.

(Lev. 26:11,12). John picks up this familiar association in his Gospel, when he says that the Word was made flesh and tabernacled among us, and we beheld His glory, the glory as of the only begotten Son of God (John 1:14). When he uses the analogy again in the Revelation, he is affirming that Emmanuel has come to abide with His people forever.

The first act of God in this new state of felicity is to wipe away all tears from the eyes of His own (21:4). All the sufferings will be gone; "sorrow and sighing will flee away" (Isa. 35:10). Recall, too, that just prior to this new creation, the church has witnessed the last judgment and final separation of those not trusting in the Lamb (20:11–15). The trauma of that experience can only be imagined—seeing persons who were loved on earth assigned to the lake of fire. It is comforting to know that God will erase the sadness of that parting from the memories of His people. Every aching heart is healed in the balm of Gilead.

So far above our present earthly experience is the glorified state, that, like the character of God, it can best be conceived in negatives. To think that there will be no more death! The last enemy of the soul has been banished; the grave has lost its sting (cf., Isa. 25:8; 2 Cor. 15:54). Neither shall there be any more mourning, nor crying, nor pain, "for the first things have passed away" (21:4). All the agonizing effects of sin are gone forever. There is not even a semblance of the raging sea; that barrier to the promised land and emblem of the world's evil order has passed away (21:1). Nothing in heaven can ever cause a tremor in the everlasting song.

## Beauty of the City

As John takes a closer look at the bridal-bedecked city, he observes that it is resplendent with "the glory of God" (21:9–11), an allusion to the all-encompassing divine Presence (cf. Ezk. 43:5). It brings to mind Isaiah's promise: "Arise, shine; for your light has come, And the glory of the

Lord has risen upon you" (Isa. 60:1; cf., Isa. 60:2,19). The brilliant light issuing from the saints is likened to the radiance of crystal-clear jasper, a beautiful hue associated with the nature of God (4:3).

The same precious stone makes up the wall encompassing the glorious Presence. Measuring 144 cubits, or 72 yards, it conveys a sense of security for those within (21:12,17,18). Though the size of the wall is not large, compared to the height of the city which it surrounds, still it is too high to scale through one's own ability, making access possible only through the proper entrances. Suggestive, too, is the multiple number of twelve, which speaks of the heavenly communion of God's people. This is further reflected by the foundations of the wall, which are inlaid with jewels that parallel roughly the twelve gems in the breastplate of the High Priest (21:19, 20; cf., Ex. 28:17–20).[4]

In the wall are twelve gates, each composed of a single pearl (21:12,21), expressive of the entrance into the kingdom through the redeeming blood of Christ.[5] The gates are arranged in three groups, separately open to the east, the north, the south, and the west, for the Gospel reaches to all people and nations; and the gates will never be closed (21:12,13,25). Stationed at the gates are twelve sentinel angels, the ministering servants of God, and written on the gates are the

---

[4] R. H. Charles points out a correlation between these jewels and the twelve signs of the Zodiac, though, in this instance, they are arranged in the reverse order of the path of the sun. He deduces from this that John is showing that the city of God has no similarity with the heathen speculations about a heavenly city. R. H. Charles, *The Revelation of St. John* II, International Critical Commentary (Edinburgh: T & T Clark, 1920), pp. 165–169. Leon Morris sees in the listing a complete repudiation of human judgment, *op. cit.*, p. 252.

[5] The pearl is made from a secretion in an oyster, to protect an injury. Without a wound, there would be no pearl. A pearl thus furnishes a fitting emblem of the Saviour by whose wounds we have obtained redemption (cf. Matt. 13:46).

names of the twelve tribes of the sons of Israel, the heirs of
the covenant (21:12; cf., Ezk. 48:30–34). Inscribed on the
foundation stones of the wall are the names of the twelve
apostles of the Lamb, underscoring the faith and mission of
the church (21:14). By engraving both the names of the tribes
and the apostles upon the city's structure, God again brings
into beautiful focus the unity of His work throughout history.

Careful attention is given to the fact that the city lies four-
square, "its length and width and height are equal" (21:16),
doubtless an allusion to the cubelike architecture of the Holy
of Holies (1 Kings 6:20). Yet, in contrast to the small cubicle
of the earth's sanctuary, the new Jerusalem measures 12,000
furlongs on each side, the equivalent of about 1500 miles, or
2,250,000 square miles, an immensity of fantastic propor-
tions. There is surely room for everyone. When the dimensions of the city are seen, too, as an infinite multiple of the
number 12, with the measurement in furlongs on all twelve
edges being 144,000, one can see how everything symbolically magnifies the perfection of God's provision for His
bride.

Intensifying the immaculate splendor is the "pure gold,
like pure glass" of which the city is made (21:18). Even the
streets are "pure gold, like transparent glass" (21:21). Nothing about it can hinder the transfusion of the glory of God.
These construction materials, of gold, pearls, and precious
jewels, among the most valuable substances known, convey a
feeling of indescribable affluence and costliness. The treasures of this world heaped together pale into nothing, by
comparison.

## Faith Becomes Sight

Even more striking is the absence of a temple in the city
(cf., Ezk. 40:1; Ezk. 46:24). The physical symbol of God's
dwelling has been replaced by the spiritual reality itself—
"for the Lord God, the Almighty, and the Lamb, are its tem-

ple" (21:22). The time has come when all who worship God, do so in spirit and truth (cf. John 4:21).

Moreover, "The city has no need of the sun or of the moon to shine upon it" (21:23; cf., 21:25). Secondary means of light are superfluous, "for the glory of the Lord has illumined it, and its lamp is the Lamb" (21:23; cf., 22:5). "And the nations shall walk by its light, and the kings of the earth shall bring their glory into it" (21:24,26). What we now see only through a glass in shadows, will then be seen in the full light of day. Communion will be direct. We shall see His face (22:4).

This life in the glorious presence of God, constantly sustained by His ever-present Spirit, is depicted by a sparkling, pure river of water proceeding out of the throne. God is sometimes described as "the fountain of living waters" (Jer. 2:13; cf., Psa. 36:9), welling up into eternal life (John 4:14). The waters in heaven nourish twelve trees of life along the banks of the stream, which bear perpetual fruit to bring healing, immortality, and growth to the nations (22:1,2; cf., Gen. 2:9; Gen. 33:22; Ezk. 47:12). That the saints will continually partake of this life-giving fruit indicates again that they are always dependent upon divine grace. We never get a hint that life comes as the result of human accomplishment—it ever flows out of God.

In the strength He gives, "His bond-servants shall serve Him" (22:3). There is no idleness in heaven. All persons, according to their gifts, will always minister to the glory of the Lord. In token of the character of Him whom they serve, "His name shall be on their foreheads" (22:4). And in the light of His countenance, as joint heirs with the King, "they shall reign forever and ever" (22:5).

## All Invited

"He who overcomes shall inherit these things," declares "the Alpha and the Omega, the beginning and the end," adding, "and I will be His God and he will be My son" (21:6,7).

The promise catches up the blessings held out to the seven churches. "To him who overcomes, I will grant to eat of the tree of life, which is in the Paradise of God" (2:7). "He who overcomes shall not be hurt by the second death" (2:11). "To him who overcomes, to him I will give . . . a white stone, and a new name written on the stone which no one knows but he who receives it" (2:17). "He who overcomes, and he who keeps My deeds until the end, to him I will give authority over the nations; and I will give him the morning star" (2: 26,28). "He who overcomes shall thus be clothed in white garments . . . and I will confess his name before My Father, and before His angels" (3:5). "He who overcomes . . . I will write upon him the name of My God, and the name of the city of My God, the new Jerusalem" (3:12). "He who overcomes, I will grant to him to sit down with Me on My throne, as I also overcame and sat down with My Father on His throne" (3:21).

All these blessings belong to the inhabitants of the holy city. But until then, there is a battle to fight, an enemy to defeat, a world system of evil to overcome. Believers must exercise their faith in undaunted obedience to the Word of God. The blessed are those who keep His commandments, "that they may have the right to the tree of life, and may enter by the gates into the city" (22:14).

The invitation is to all. God wants no one to miss it. And since salvation has already been procured through the blood of Christ, He says, "I will give to the one who thirsts from the spring of the water of life without cost" (21:6). So "the Spirit and the bride say, 'Come.' And let the one who hears say, 'Come.' And let the one who is thirsty come"; and whosoever will, let him come and drink freely from the wellsprings of everlasting life (22:17). As Charles Wesley sang:

> Thou of life the fountain art
> Freely let me take of Thee,

Spring Thou up within my heart,
Rise to all eternity.

## The Journey Ended

I will never forget my dad, one day before he died, turning to me and asking, "Where does a man go when he goes out with God?"

The question came as such a surprise that I was a bit confused. Seeing my perplexity, Dad smiled, then in a quiet voice, said: "Does it matter? You just go wherever He wants to go."

He was thinking of that passage which says of Abraham, "When he was called, obeyed by going out to a place which he was to receive for an inheritance; and he went out, not knowing where he was going. By faith he lived as an alien in the land of promise, as in a foreign land, dwelling in tents with Isaac and Jacob, fellow-heirs of the same promise; for he was looking for the city which has foundations, whose architect and builder is God" (Heb. 11:8–10).

That is the way it is with everyone who has obeyed the voice from above. Once we have been called to go "out," we know that we can never be satisfied to stay in the old country. God has something better for us. It really does not make any difference where we go, as long as we are together, for where He is, there is heaven. Following Him, we have perfect peace. Our part is simply to trust and obey. In this pilgrimage of faith, we are content to live as aliens in this world, "as in a foreign land," for we have been spoiled by the vision of another world, "a city which has foundations, whose architect and builder is God."

The vision gets brighter as we near the other shore, though there will be obstacles to overcome until the very end. In his inimitable way, Bunyan observed that as Christian and Hopeful approached the celestial city, they saw a river between them and the gate. Finding no bridge over the water, they started wading across. But Christian's faith began to falter, and he cried out to his friend, "I sink in deep water; the billows go over my head." Hopeful, however, supported by the Word of God, answered, "Be of good cheer, my brother, I feel the bottom, and it is good." Then, looking ahead, he exclaimed: "I see the gate! I see the gate! And men standing by to receive us." Encouraged by this assurance, Christian, too, rested upon the promises, whereupon he found ground to stand, and soon crossed the river.

They were met on the other side by some of the shining host, who compassed them round on every side, forming an escort to the King. As they entered through the gates, the celestial choirs filled heaven with melodious music. There was singing and shouting and the sounding of trumpets. And all the bells of the city rang with joy.[6]

With this homecoming growing closer for every pilgrim, let us not be disobedient to the heavenly vision. Soon the journey will be over. Each step we take brings us nearer to the Father's house, when the gates open wide and the familiar voice is heard, "Come, My blessed. Enter into your Master's joy." As the trumpets sound and the bells of the city ring, we shall then join the resplendent throng about the throne and sing the praise of Him who is worthy, our loving Saviour and Lord, until time shall wane and be no more.

This is the reality in which the Christian lives. Though our body is still held by the earth, our spirit can soar with the angels in the city of unceasing song. There we are at home. In the inner sanctuary of our being, we are already beginning to know something of that worship in which the King of heaven dwells. And the singing grows sweeter with the years.

---

[6] John Bunyan, *The Pilgrim's Progress* (New York: Peter Pauper Press), pp. 149–154.

All creatures of our God and King,
Lift up your voice and with us sing
    Alleluia, Alleluia!
Thou burning sun with golden beam,
Thou silver moon with softer gleam:
        O Praise Him, O praise Him,
        Alleluia, Alleluia, Alleluia!

And all ye men of tender heart
Forgiving others, to be your part,
    O sing ye! Alleluia!
Ye who long pain and sorrow bear,
Praise God and on Him cast your care!
        O praise Him! O praise Him!
        Alleluia! Alleluia! Alleluia!

And then, most kind and gentle death,
Waiting to hush our latest breath,
    O praise Him! Alleluia!
Thou leadest home the child of God
And Christ our Lord the way hath trod.
        O praise Him! O praise Him!
        Alleluia! Alleluia! Alleluia!

Let all things their creator bless,
And worship Him in humbleness,
    O praise Him, Alleluia!
Praise, praise the Father, praise the Son,
And praise the Spirit, Three in One!
        O praise Him, O praise Him,
        Alleluia, Alleluia, Alleluia!

FRANCIS OF ASSISI
tr. BY WILLIAM H. DRAPER